Walnut Canyon National Monument
Geologic Resource Evaluation Report

Natural Resource Report NPS/NRPC/GRD/NRR—2008/040

Geologic Resources Division
Natural Resource Program Center
P.O. Box 25287
Denver, Colorado 80225

June 2008

U.S. Department of the Interior
Washington, D.C.

The Natural Resource Publication series addresses natural resource topics that are of interest and applicability to a broad readership in the National Park Service and to others in the management of natural resources, including the scientific community, the public, and the NPS conservation and environmental constituencies. Manuscripts are peer- reviewed to ensure that the information is scientifically credible, technically accurate, appropriately written for the intended audience, and is designed and published in a professional manner.

Natural Resource Reports are the designated medium for disseminating high priority, current natural resource management information with managerial application. The series targets a general, diverse audience, and may contain NPS policy considerations or address sensitive issues of management applicability. Examples of the diverse array of reports published in this series include vital signs monitoring plans; "how to" resource management papers; proceedings of resource management workshops or conferences; annual reports of resource programs or divisions of the Natural Resource Program Center; resource action plans; fact sheets; and regularly- published newsletters.

Views and conclusions in this report are those of the authors and do not necessarily reflect policies of the National Park Service. Mention of trade names or commercial products does not constitute endorsement or recommendation for use by the National Park Service.

Printed copies of reports in these series may be produced in a limited quantity and they are only available as long as the supply lasts. This report is also available from the Geologic Resource Evaluation Program website (http://www2.nature.nps.gov/geology/inventory/gre_publications) on the internet, or by sending a request to the address on the back cover. Please cite this publication as:

Graham, J. 2008. Walnut Canyon National Monument Geologic Resource Evaluation Report. Natural Resource Report NPS/NRPC/GRD/NRR—2008/•••. National Park Service, Denver, Colorado.

NPS D- 38, June 2008

Table of Contents

List of Figures

List of Tables

Executive Summary

This report accompanies the digital geologic map for Walnut Canyon National Monument in Arizona, which the Geologic Resources Division produced in collaboration with its partners. It contains information relevant to resource management and scientific research.

Walnut Canyon National Monument was established in 1915 to protect and preserve the cliff dwellings of the Sinagua culture. The Sinagua occupied the region from about 1100 to 1220 A.D., and constructed their dwellings in alcoves eroded into relatively soft sandstone layers beneath harder, resistant limestone ledges. The cliff dwellings are in the upper third of Walnut Canyon, which Walnut Creek has incised into relatively horizontal layers of Paleozoic limestone and sandstone.

The primary geologic issue facing Walnut Canyon resource management is rockfall. Rockfall is a natural process that has shaped Walnut Canyon for thousands of years. However, rockfall can have a significant impact on visitor and staff safety, park infrastructure, and archaeological resources in the park. There is a specific hazard within the canyon along the Island Trail where climate related factors contribute to the timing of rockfall events. In addition, large, angular blocks of limestone from the Kaibab Formation have narrowed the canyon floor in places.

Another important geologic resource management issue is the combined geomorphic and hydrogeologic response to decreased water flow in Walnut Creek. Decreased sediment input reduced streambed scouring and recharge from alluvial aquifers. In the monument, approximately 80 acres of riparian vegetation grows on the floor of Walnut Canyon. Loss of this native vegetation because of decreased flows would not only eliminate the riparian landscape, indicative of the natural setting at the time of the Sinagua, but also negatively impact the viewshed from primary visitor use areas.

Two dam impoundments upstream of Walnut Creek have altered the character of the stream, the riparian ecosystem, and the limited water resources within the monument. The impoundment and diversion of Walnut Creek since 1941 have negatively affected wetland, floodplain, and riparian habitats that depend on a scoured channel, periodic flooding, and available groundwater. To help assess the sustainability of the riparian corridor within Walnut Canyon, field studies and baseline documentation are needed to identify and monitor geomorphic changes and groundwater flow.

Other geologic issues include volcanic eruptions, seismicity, mass wasting, flash flooding, potential aquifer contamination, and fossil theft. Approximately 1,000 years ago, volcanic eruptions produced the Sunset Crater in the San Francisco volcanic field north of Walnut Canyon. Future eruptions that would produce volcanic ash and cinders are possible, but not predictable with current technology. Earthquakes along local normal faults pose only a minor threat to the infrastructure and archaeological resources at the park. However, the Anderson Mesa fault and the smaller Marshall Lake fault, both located south of the monument, show evidence of recent movement.

Although stream flow has decreased in Walnut Creek, flash flooding remains a potential hazard. Intense thunderstorms may produce flash floods from local tributary canyons. Flooding in Walnut Canyon would also occur if either of the two upstream dams were to catastrophically fail.

Fossils are present in the limestone ledges of the Kaibab Formation outcrop along park trails making them vulnerable to theft. The majority of the paleontological resources at Walnut Canyon are marine invertebrates. Spiral impressions of snails, molds of small clams, and brachiopods are the most common fossils along the trails.

The porous Coconino Sandstone is an important regional aquifer in northern Arizona and provides the only reliable groundwater beneath the monument at a depth of approximately 460 m (1,500 ft). The National Park Service maintains a well into the aquifer, and the water table has remained relatively stable. Under current conditions, there is little threat of contamination or aquifer depletion within the watershed. However, the city of Flagstaff has annexed all lands to the north and west of the monument boundary and any development there could significantly increase non- point source pollution in perched aquifers, springs, and seeps that flow into the canyon.

Introduction

The following section briefly describes the National Park Service Geologic Resource Evaluation Program and the regional geologic setting of Walnut Canyon National Monument.

Purpose of the Geologic Resources Evaluation Program

The Geologic Resource Evaluation (GRE) Program is one of 12 inventories funded under the NPS Natural Resource Challenge designed to enhance baseline information available to park managers. The program carries out the geologic component of the inventory effort from the development of digital geologic maps to providing park staff with a geologic report tailored to a park's specific geologic resource issues. The Geologic Resources Division of the Natural Resource Program Center administers this program. The GRE team relies heavily on partnerships with the U.S. Geological Survey, Colorado State University, state surveys, and others in developing GRE products.

The goal of the GRE Program is to increase understanding of the geologic processes at work in parks and provide sound geologic information for use in park decision making. Sound park stewardship relies on understanding natural resources and their role in the ecosystem. Geology is the foundation of park ecosystems. The compilation and use of natural resource information by park managers is called for in section 204 of the National Parks Omnibus Management Act of 1998 and in NPS- 75, Natural Resources Inventory and Monitoring Guideline.

To realize this goal, the GRE team is systematically working towards providing each of the identified 270 natural area parks with a geologic scoping meeting, a digital geologic map, and a geologic report. These products support the stewardship of park resources and are designed for non- geoscientists. During scoping meetings the GRE team brings together park staff and geologic experts to review available geologic maps and discuss specific geologic issues, features, and processes.

The GRE mapping team converts the geologic maps identified for park use at the scoping meeting into digital geologic data in accordance with their innovative Geographic Information Systems (GIS) Data Model. These digital data sets bring an exciting interactive dimension to traditional paper maps by providing geologic data for use in park GIS and facilitating the incorporation of geologic considerations into a wide range of resource management applications. The newest maps come complete with interactive help files. As a companion to the digital geologic maps, the GRE team prepares a park- specific geologic report that aids in use of the maps and provides park managers with an overview of park geology and geologic resource management issues.

For additional information regarding the content of this report and up to date GRE contact information please refer to the Geologic Resource Evaluation Web site (http://www2.nature.nps.gov/geology/inventory/).

Location and Regional Setting

Walnut Canyon National Monument is located approximately 11 km (7 mi) east of Flagstaff, Arizona. The monument was established in 1915 to protect the areas natural resources and ancient Native American ruins that date from about 1100 to 1220 A.D. Access to the monument is by a paved road to the northern rim of Walnut Canyon from Interstate- 40 and by various unpaved roads from the adjacent Coconino National Forest, managed by the U.S. Forest Service (fig. 1). The park road ends at a visitor center on the northern rim of the canyon. Island and Rim trails are the only two hiking trails managed and maintained by Walnut Canyon National Monument (fig. 2). Public use is limited to these designated trails and adjacent picnic areas (NPS 2003; Hansen et al. 2004).

The monument covers 3,579.46 acres and ranges in elevation from 1,890 to 2,100 m (6,200 to 6,900 ft). The stream and canyon are named after the Arizona walnut trees that grow along the floor of the canyon (Vandiver 1936; NPS 2003).

A moderately hot and moist summer, cool and dry spring and fall, and cold, periodically wet, winter typify the semi- arid, continental climate of Walnut Canyon National Monument (Hansen et al. 2004). Average annual precipitation at the monument headquarters is approximately 51 centimeters (cm) (20 in) (Thomas 2003). Monsoon- like precipitation events occur principally from July through September, often in the form of intense thunderstorms of short duration.

Regional Geology

Walnut Canyon National Monument is part of the Colorado Plateau Physiographic Province consisting of high plateaus, deep narrow canyons, and broad, rounded uplands covering an area of 83,200,000 acres in northern Arizona, northwestern New Mexico, western Colorado, and southeastern Utah. To the south, the Colorado Plateau ends abruptly along the Mogollon Rim, a roughly 320 km (200 mile) long, faulted escarpment that cuts across much of central Arizona.

The main geologic and topographic feature of Walnut Canyon National Monument is Walnut Canyon, an entrenched segment of Walnut Creek. The canyon trends from west to east and is incised into the Coconino

Plateau that extends from the South Rim of the Grand Canyon to Flagstaff. Walnut Canyon averages 402 m (1,320 ft) wide from the north rim to the south rim, 122 m (400 ft) deep at the western (upstream) boundary, and 76 m (250 ft) deep at the eastern (downstream) boundary. Anderson Mesa rises above the Coconino Plateau south of Walnut Canyon (fig. 3). Cherry Canyon is a major drainage to the southeast of Walnut Canyon.

The resistant gray limestone of the Permian Kaibab Formation caps the upper walls of Walnut Canyon (fig. 5). This same formation forms the rims of Grand Canyon and the higher, relatively flat mesas surrounding the narrow canyon within the monument. Locally, more than 111 m (364 ft) of massive, resistant limestone and dolomite of the Kaibab interbedded with thin, less resistant siltstones and sandstones form characteristic ledges and slopes. The ancient dwellings in Walnut Canyon were constructed under the shelter of overhanging ledges of Kaibab limestone 61 m (200 ft) or more above the canyon bottom (fig. 4).

The light- tan Permian Coconino Sandstone underlies the Kaibab Formation (fig. 5). The Coconino Sandstone is a distinctive cross- bedded sandstone unit that formed when the regression of an ancient sea exposed vast tracts of sand to prevailing winds , blowing the sand into large dune fields similar to the modern Sahara. In this area of the Colorado Plateau, the massive cross- bedded sandstones of the Coconino are difficult to differentiate from cross- bedded sandstones of the overlying Toroweap Formation, and so they are mapped as one unit in Walnut Canyon area. However, careful field examination reveals that a truncation surface marked by vegetation in outcrop exposures typically separates Toroweap beds from the underlying Coconino Sandstone (Turner 2003). Within Walnut Canyon, the combined Coconino and Toroweap unit is 225 m (738 ft) thick (Rowlands et al. 1995).

The Coconino Sandstone is the primary aquifer in the region. Local fractures, parting along bedding planes, and limestone dissolution allows precipitation to percolate through the Kaibab Formation to the underlying Coconino Sandstone recharging this regional aquifer (Paul Whitefield, NPS WACA, written communication November 30, 2005).

Uplift of the Colorado Plateau in the Cenozoic Era and regional erosion removed most of the Mesozoic and Cenozoic rocks from the Walnut Creek area. Although the siltstones, mudstones, and sandstones of the Triassic Moenkopi Formation have been mostly eroded, they do outcrop locally, ranging in thickness from 0 to 120 m (0 to 394 ft) (Rowlands et al. 1995). Patchy outcrops occur along the upthrown side of the Anderson Mesa normal fault. The Moenkopi also outcrops in narrow structural basins oblique to the Anderson Mesa Fault in Walnut Canyon.

Tertiary and Quaternary basaltic lava flows locally cap the sedimentary strata. The Anderson Mesa Basalt caps

Anderson Mesa immediately south of Walnut Canyon (fig. 3). Basaltic lava flows within the Lake Mary Graben are approximately 38 m (125 ft) thick, covered by Quaternary alluvium (Rowlands et al. 1995). Like the Kaibab Formation, these fractured basalts act as recharge zones for many local perched aquifers.

Quaternary alluvial (stream) and lacustrine (lake) deposits are as thick as 23 m (75 ft) (Rowlands et al. 1995). Colluvial (slope) deposits of talus at the base of slopes occur along the downthrown sides of faults, in canyons, and along margins of lava flows.

Faults and fractures that strike perpendicular to the trend of Walnut Canyon across Anderson Mesa and along the Lower Lake Mary shoreline are the dominate the geologic structures of the area (fig. 3). The major fault is the Anderson Mesa Fault - a normal fault that forms the southwest boundary of Anderson Mesa and the northeast boundary of the Lake Mary basin (Rowlands et al. 1995).

Park History

The earliest evidence of humans living in Walnut Canyon dates back to 4,000 B.C. (Hansen et al. 2004). However, the highest density of prehistoric people living in the area was from 600 A.D. to 1250 A.D. when a prehistoric farming culture flourished in the Flagstaff area (Hansen et al. 2004; http://www.nps.gov/waca/index.htm, accessed October, 2004). The Spanish named these people the Sinagua culture, a name taken from "Sierra Sinagua" meaning "mountain range without water" (NPS 2003; Hansen et al. 2004; http://nps.gov/waca/index.htm, accessed October 2004). Although Noble (1991) refers to the "Sinagua Indians," Sinagua is not the name of a tribe or clan, but refers to various archeological sites and objects found in this part of Arizona that have similar characteristics. How these people collectively perceived themselves and their neighbors, or what they called themselves is not known (http://www.nps.gov/waca, accessed October, 2004).

The ancient farmers grew corn, squash, and beans above the Walnut Canyon rim. Ash and cinders from the eruptions of nearby Sunset Crater Volcano (the last eruption occurred about 1,000 years ago) enriched the soil, curbed evaporation, conserved soil moisture, and increased productivity of the Sinagua's fields so that the regional population began to grow. People first moved down into the canyon about 1150 A.D. when they built most of the cliff dwellings that line the canyon walls. Although little water flows in Walnut Creek today because of two upstream dams, Walnut Creek once supported a rich variety of plants and animals (http://nps.gov/waca, accessed October 2004).

The Sinagua culture in Walnut Canyon thrived for about 150 years, but around 1250 A.D., the Sinagua mysteriously abandoned the canyon. Archaeologists are not sure why the Sinagua people left, but probable causes include lack of precipitation, falling water tables, permanent water shortages, resource depletion, repeated crop failures, and rapidly expanding arroyo systems (Schroeder 1977; Rowlands et al. 1995; http://www.desertusa.com/ind1/du_peo_sin.html, accessed March 2007). Hopi oral histories tell of the Sinagua migrations (http://www.desertusa.com /ind1 /du_peo_sin.html, accessed March 2007; Noble 1991).

The Walnut Canyon cliff dwellings are unique in that they are the only known such remains of the northern Sinagua culture. The site density in the monument averages almost 100 sites per square mile, compared with typical densities of 40 sites per square mile in other areas near Flagstaff (NPS 2003). About 300 rooms are scattered along both sides of Walnut Canyon. In 1885, James Stevenson of the Smithsonian Institution visited the area and noted,

> "The doors are large and extend from the ground up to a sufficient height to admit a man without stooping. The rooms are large and the walls are two to four feet thick. The fireplaces are in one corner of the room on an elevated rock, and the smoke can only escape through the door. The masonry compares favorably with the construction of the best villages in Canyon de Chelly. Many objects of interest were found in the debris around and in these houses. Matting, sandals, spindle whorls, and stone implements of various kinds abound."
>
> (Vandiver 1936, p. 2).

Vandals and thieves removed almost all of the archaeological objects from the cliff dwellings described by Stevenson, and many of the cliff dwellings were broken down and destroyed prior to 1906 when the U.S. Forest Service first protected the area (Vandiver 1936). The dense concentration of prehistoric ruins, their exceptional state of preservation, and their unusual and highly scenic setting in sheltered alcoves, as well as the threat of imminent destruction by commercial looters and misguided tourists were key factors influencing the creation of Walnut Canyon National Monument (NPS 2003).

No large settlements of humans inhabited Walnut Canyon after 1250 A.D., but the surrounding landscape has been altered by historic and modern human activity such as logging, hunting, fire suppression, housing development, water impoundments, and road and utility construction. In 1973, the park installed a fences around protected ruins and prohibited livestock grazing. Grazing continues in areas adjacent to the monument and within the unfenced monument boundary (Hansen et al. 2004).

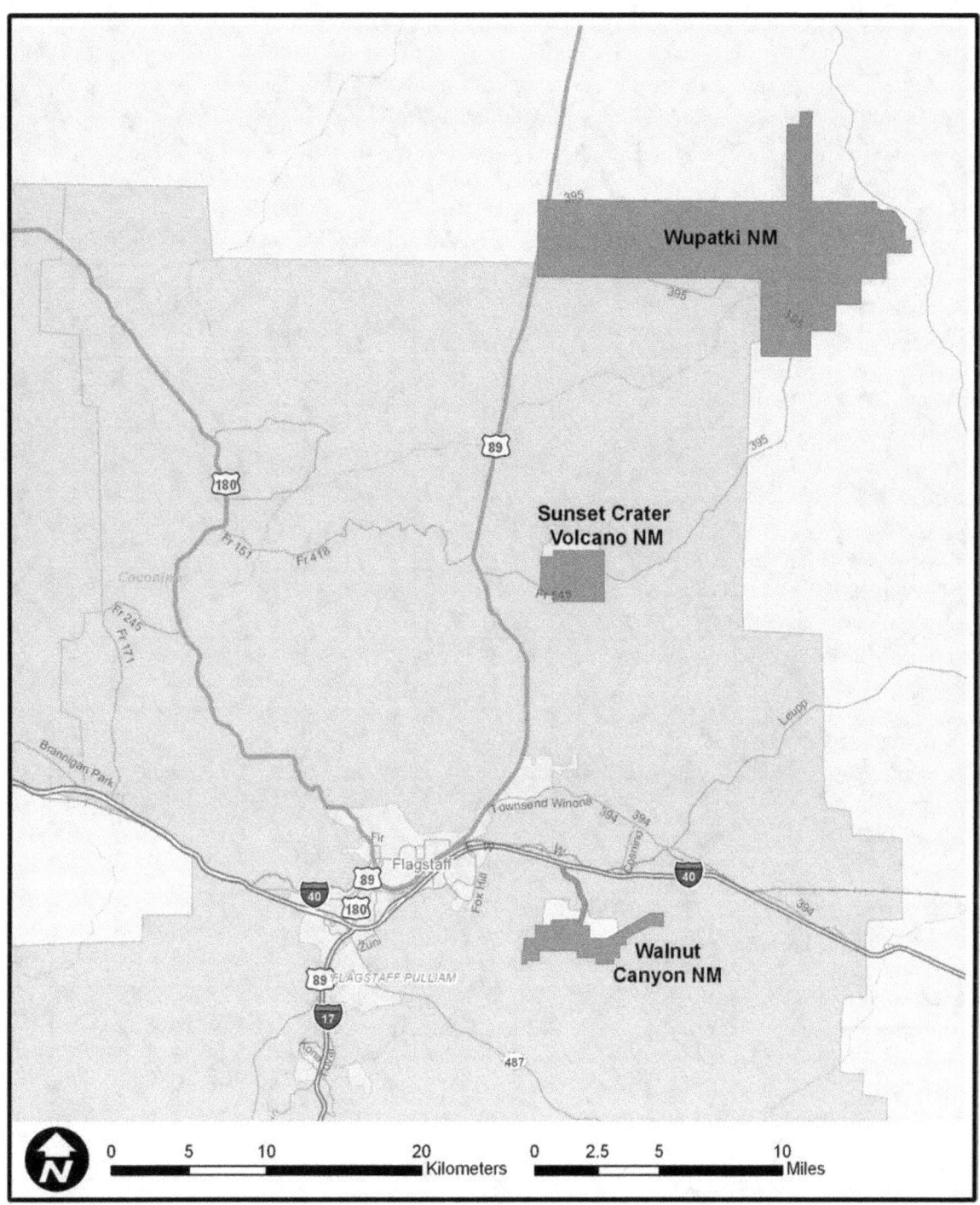

Figure 1. Regional location map for Walnut Canyon National Monument.

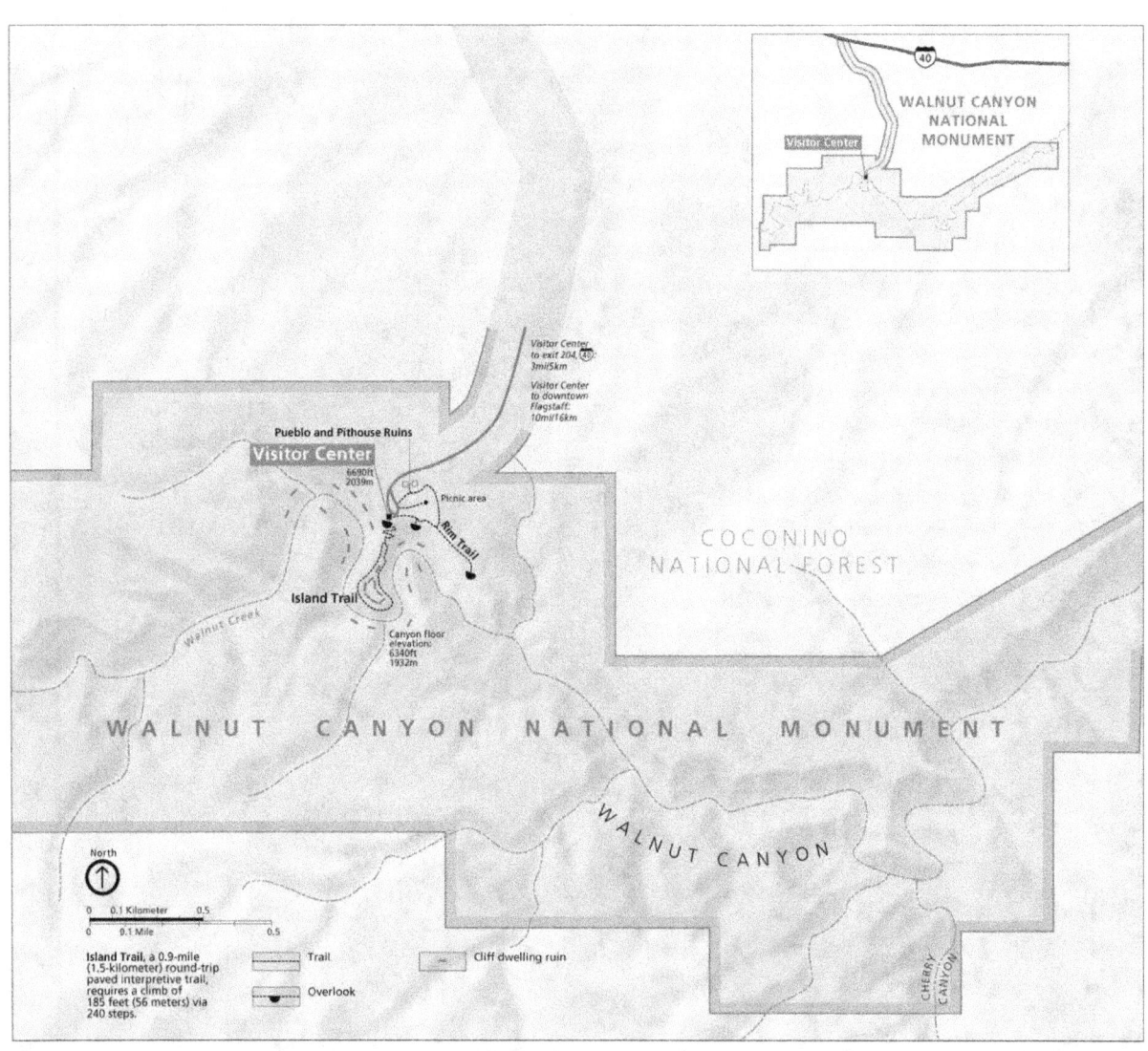

Figure 2 Trails and relief in Walnut Canyon National Monument. Map courtesy of the National Park Service, http://www.nps.gov/waca/planyourvisit/index.htm (Accessed March 2007).

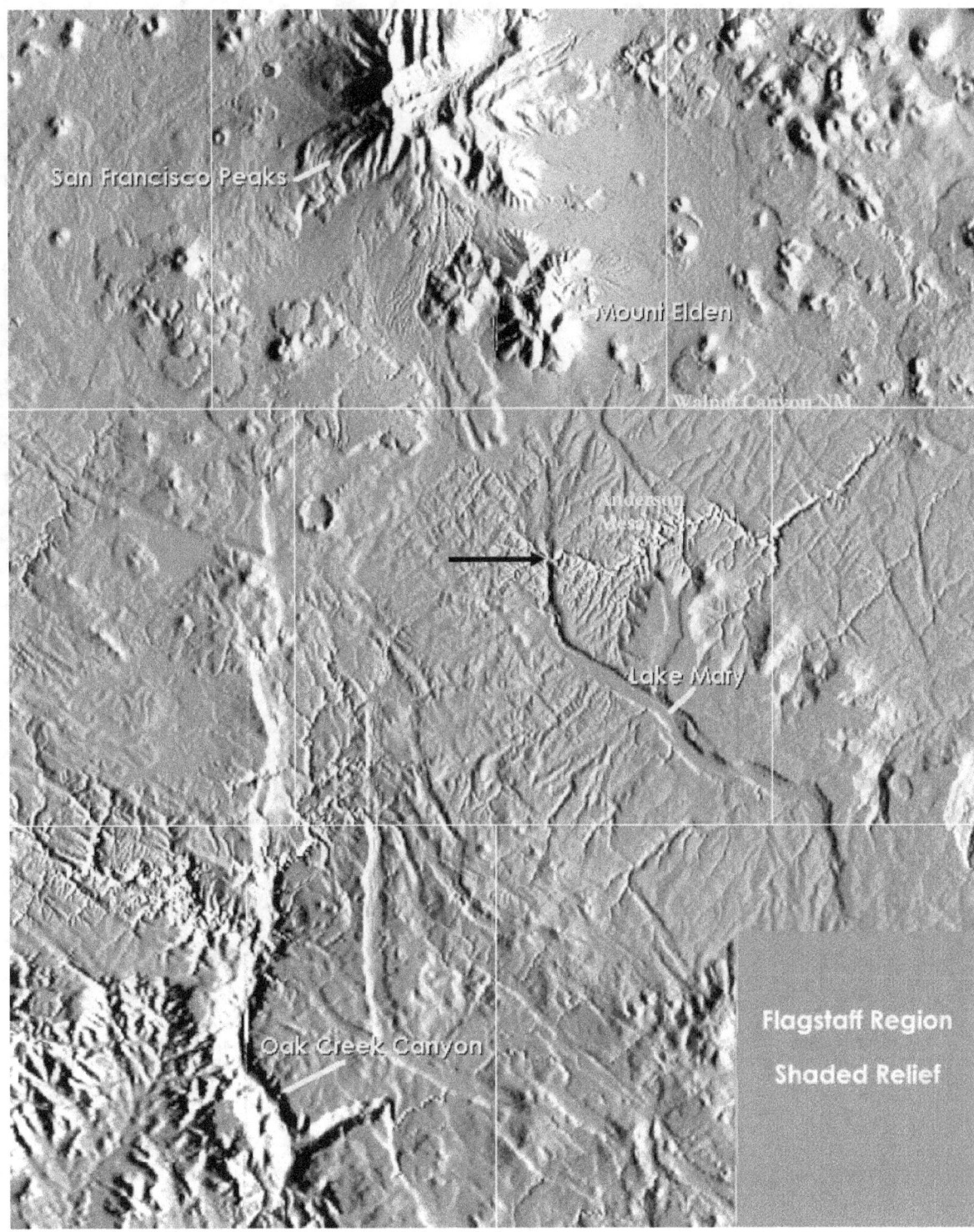

Figure 3. Shaded relief map showing the Walnut Canyon National Monument area. The black arrow points to the escarpment of the Anderson Mesa Fault. Lake Mary lies in the graben formed by the fault. The north-south lineaments that cross Walnut Canyon and the northwest-southeast and northeast-southwest features are faults. The image was generated using 30 meter resolution Digital Elevation Model (DEM) data. Map courtesy of the U.S. Geological Survey, http://terraweb.wr.usgs.gov/projects/Flagstaff/ dem.html (Accessed March 2007).

Figure 4. Cliff dwellings at Walnut Canyon National Monument constructed in an alcove within the Kaibab Formation beneath an overhanging ledge of limestone. Photo courtesy of the USGS; http://3dparks.wr.usgs.gov/walnutcanyon/html2/wc1650.htm (Accessed March 6, 2007).

Period	Formation/Unit	General Lithology
Quaternary	Alluvium	Unconsolidated gravel, sand, silt deposits
	Lacustrine deposits	Fine- grained lake deposits
	Colluvium	Unconsolidated gravel, sand, & basalt
Regional Unconformity		
Triassic	Moenkopi Fm	Mudstone, siltstone, & sandstone
Regional Unconformity		
Permian	Kaibab Fm.	Dolomite, sandy limestone, cherty limestone
	Toroweap Fm. & Coconino Sandstone	Cross- bedded quartz sandstone
Regional Unconformity		
Pennsylvanian/Permian	Supai Group	Not exposed in Walnut Canyon NM

Figure 5. Generalized stratigraphic column for Walnut Canyon National Monument, Arizona.

Geologic Issues

A Geologic Resource Evaluation scoping session was held for Walnut Canyon National Monument on June 28–29, 2001, to discuss geologic resources, address the status of geologic mapping, and assess resource management issues and needs. The following section synthesizes the scoping results, in particular those issues that may require attention from resource managers.

Since 1941, flow in Walnut Creek has been severely limited due to two upstream dams. Decreased flow has resulted in reduced sediment input, reduced streambed scouring, reduced recharge of springs and seeps, and a more static channel morphology. Changes in the geomorphic and hydrogeologic character of the canyon bottom and Walnut Creek have caused changes in the riparian habitat flanking the creek, which depends on a scoured channel, periodic flooding, and adequate groundwater. The riparian areas in Walnut Canyon provide an important element of the desired cultural landscape setting for the Sinagua cliff dwellings and enhances the natural viewshed from the primary visitor use areas. Ultimately, the riparian corridor significantly enhances habitat diversity, species richness, cultural resource integrity, and visitor experience (Whitefield 2005). For these reasons, defining the integrated geomorphic and hydrogeologic response to decreased water flow in the canyon is the primary geologic issue facing Walnut Canyon National Monument.

Rockfall

Rockfall is a serious hazard in the rugged canyons of Walnut Canyon National Monument that can impact visitor and staff safety as well as park infrastructure. The Island Trail is the most popular trail at Walnut Canyon National Monument. It descends into a steep, rugged canyon allowing park visitors to hike in a natural environment and view ancient cliff dwellings. On November 30th and December 8th, 2007 two rockfalls damaged large sections of the Island Trail. The initial rockfall blocked the lower section of the trail and the much larger December 8th event took out large sections of a concrete stairway, steel handrails, and a bench. As a result the trail is closed to visitor use pending remediation (Greco 2008).

The natural processes that formed the canyon are still at work and can sometimes produce hazardous conditions. Climate can be a primary driver behind hazards in Walnut Canyon as was the case with recent events. The weathering and erosion of material from slopes is seasonally controlled. Extreme mechanical weathering from freeze- thaw action during the winter months can account for a large portion of the debris moving down slope. During climatic extremes such as drought, heavy snow pack or extreme rainstorms, the erosion cycles can be accelerated. In times of drought, excess debris builds up, then during rainstorms events or snow melt, the amount of material flushed can increase substantially (Greco 2008).

The 2007 rockfall events were not unique in Walnut Canyon National Monument. Rockfall is a natural occurance and a long history of past rockfalls is evident in the talus and large boulders scattered throughout the canyon. Scars on the canyon walls likewise identify where large chunks of rock have previously fallen. Larger size rockfalls occur infrequently and are only addressed when they impact park infrastructure or threaten visitor. Smaller rockfalls occur much more frequently and usually go unreported.

Geomorphology and Hydrogeology

Walnut Canyon National Monument contains 13 linear km (8 linear mi) of Walnut Canyon. The canyon bottom is narrowly- incised into the Coconino Sandstone where the Walnut Creek drainage meanders northeastward through coarse- grained stream terrace deposits and talus blocks from the canyon walls. Water catchment basins of various sizes, scoured into the Coconino Sandstone, provide important water sources for wildlife. Groundwater from numerous fractures and bedding planes seeps from the steep canyon walls and tributary canyons (Chronic 1983; NPS 2003; Whitefield 2005).

The Walnut Canyon watershed drains an area of about 108,800 acres or 170 square miles (440 sq km). Approximately 75%, or 83,200 acres, 130 square miles, (337 sq km) of the Walnut Creek watershed lies upstream of the monument to the south and west in the Coconino National Forest. Walnut Creek headwaters originate in the Mormon Mountain- Mormon Lakes area more than 32 km (20 mi) south of the monument. Prior to the first upstream dam construction in 1904, anecdotal and photographic evidence suggests that Walnut Creek was once an ephemeral stream with an open, rocky bed maintained by seasonal flooding (Rowlands et al. 1995). Reliable flows typically occurred early each year during the seasonal spring snowmelt. Less predictable flows occurred during the summer and fall thunderstorm season. Today, dense stands of invasive, hearty upland woody vegetation choke the bottom of Walnut Creek (Rowlands et al. 1995).

Wetlands, floodplains, and riparian habitats covering about 90 acres within Walnut Canyon National Monument are restricted to the narrow canyon bottom and a number of perennial seeps found in the tributary canyons on the south side of the monument. Riparian vegetation includes a tree canopy of box elder, Arizona walnut, narrow- leaf cottonwood, Rocky Mountain juniper, ponderosa pine, Douglas fir, and Gambel oak.

The understory contains red osier dogwood, New Mexico locust, wild grape, Arizona wild rose, fragrant sumac, and snowberry. The riparian flora includes more than 150 species, or approximately one- third of the total flora variety within the monument (Hansen et al. 2004; Whitefield 2005). Riparian habitats are a vital component to the Walnut Canyon ecosystem.

Three dams built between 1885 and 1941 affected the geomorphology and the riparian corridor within the greater Walnut Canyon drainage. A masonry dam constructed downstream (eastern boundary of the monument) dammed lower Walnut Creek between 1883 and 1886. The reservoir supplied water to the Santa Fe Railway (Rowlands et al. 1995; NPS 2003; Whitefield 2005). The railway discontinued use of the reservoir in 1904, and in 1934, stockmen from the Kellum Ranch blasted the northern end of the dam to allow any accumulated water to drain out (Rowlands et al. 1995).

In 1990, the owner of the Santa Fe Dam repaired the dam, briefly impounding runoff during March and April 1991 (NPS 1992; Rowlands et al. 1995). Creek flow is ephemeral, but the dam still impounds some water after major flows. During rare flood events, the canyon bottom is totally inundated for about 1.6 km (1 mi) upstream of the dam. Flooding transports alluvium down the canyon which collects behind the dam. These fine sediments now mantle the canyon and have essentially filled in the "reservoir."

In 1904, construction of the first of two upstream dams created Lower Lake Mary to provide water for sawmills in Flagstaff. The lake was named for the oldest daughter of Timothy A. Riordan of the Arizona Lumber and Timber Company. This earthen dam significantly disrupted seasonal water flow through the canyon. The dam spanned a local fault zone and water infiltrated the porous and fractured bedrock along the fault.

A second earthen dam, built in 1941, created Upper Lake Mary - an important public water supply for Flagstaff. This second dam effectively ceased regular flow of Walnut Creek. While long- term hydrological data do not exist for Walnut Creek, research suggests that the impoundments have altered the frequency of flows in Walnut Canyon and have probably altered the magnitude and duration of peak flooding (Rowlands et al. 1995). Prior to upstream impoundment, winter and spring flows through Walnut Canyon occurred annually. Now, these flow events occur once every nine years on average. Summer flows from the Upper Lake Mary and Lower Lake Mary reservoirs have been completely eliminated through Walnut Canyon. Summer flows in Walnut Creek only arise from unusually heavy local runoff from canyon slopes and from tributaries below Lower Lake Mary. Estimates of annual surface water runoff into Walnut Canyon suggest a flow volume reduction from 360 million to 31 million cubic meters (290,000 to 25,000 acre- feet) due to the presence of the two upstream reservoirs (Rowlands et al. 1995). Yet to be fully understood are changes to stream channel scouring, sediment transport, alluvial terrace formation, and local spring and seep recharge, resulting from creek impoundment are (Rowlands et al. 1995; NPS 2003; Whitefield 2005).

In 1993, heavy and prolonged rains over Arizona caused the most widespread and severe flooding since the turn of the Twentieth Century (Rowlands et al. 1995). For eight weeks, floodwaters flowed through Walnut Canyon. Ephemeral drainages without dams are subject to twice- yearly seasonal runoff and are able to maintain open channels and support riparian plant species, such as willows. A true riparian ecosystem may have existed in Walnut Canyon prior to the 1904 dam construction (Rowlands et al. 1995).

The extent and volume of groundwater collection and movement within the Walnut Canyon drainage system is not known. The Coconino Sandstone is the regional aquifer beneath Walnut Canyon National Monument. The local water table of this aquifer is at least 180 m (600 ft) below the canyon floor with no potential for surface discharge. Fractures in the bedrock and dissolution of the limestone in the Kaibab Formation allow recharge of the numerous seeps at the base of the canyon walls in response to local precipitation. The seeps may flow continuously in wet years but remain dry during droughts. Persistent drought conditions since 1996 have resulted in nearly dry seeps along the base of Walnut Canyon (Whitefield 2005).

Faulting in the Kaibab Limestone, and porous Coconino Sandstone contributes to the recharge and confinement pathways in the Walnut Creek terrace deposits. Hydrogeologic characteristics in the monument favorable to local recharge include (Whitefield 2005):

- Up to 60 m (200 ft) of highly porous and permeable Kaibab limestone allowing precipitation to rapidly percolate to the underlying Coconino Sandstone aquifer. Some groundwater flows horizontally along the contact between the formations, whereas some is confined and flows laterally through local fractures and bedding planes.

- The Anderson Mesa Basalt caps Anderson Mesa and serves as a recharge zone for many small perched aquifers.

- Sedimentary strata and basalt flows dip gently to the northeast, directing lateral groundwater flow toward the southern canyon walls. This flow may be responsible for the seeps in the sandstone bedding planes at the base of the canyon.

- At least three faults as well as several minor faults and fractures strike perpendicular to Walnut Canyon. Although a considerable volume of groundwater is immediately directed to the deep Coconino Aquifer, some groundwater may move laterally through the faults and into the canyon.

- The narrow Walnut Canyon, incised into sandstone bedrock, contains shallow flanking terraces of coarse alluvium. Groundwater seeping from bedrock could collect in shallow lenses within the terrace deposits.

- Precipitation or intermittent surface flows within the local watershed below Lower Lake Mary reservoir may directly recharge the terrace deposits.

Restoring seasonal water flows of Walnut Creek is a necessary step toward total restoration of the riparian corridor within Walnut Canyon. It is unlikely that the upstream dams will be removed, but in 2001, the National Park Service, Forest Service, and City of Flagstaff agreed to cooperatively investigate methods to increase the probability of flood flows from Lower Lake Mary reservoir in order to improve the inner canyon environment (Whitefield 2005). Assessing stream channel changes over time and the potential for shallow groundwater(perched aquifers) within the corridor is fundamental to riparian ecosystem management. Understanding groundwater flow within the canyon is the first step to correlating upland vegetation and soil conditions, intermittent flows in tributary drainages, reservoir levels, and downstream groundwater fluctuations with the status of the canyon riparian corridor.

Rowlands and others (1995) characterized the vegetation changes in Walnut Canyon due to upstream impoundments, but persistent research needs include field studies to characterize the changes to channel morphology and the occurrence of shallow groundwater within the inner canyon stream terrace deposits (Paul Whitefield, NPS Natural Resource Specialist, written communication, March 29, 2007). Recommended research include (Whitefield 2005):

- Re- measure twelve stream profiles (Phillips 1990), describing the composition and geomorphology of the drainage terrace and channel deposits and compare to 1990 measurements.
- Using hand- held equipment, complete a geophysical investigation to determine the position of the groundwater table, to measure the thickness of stream terrace deposits, and to determine the subsurface contact with Coconino sandstone bedrock.
- If the geophysical investigation confirms the presence of shallow groundwater, install shallow groundwater monitoring wells.
- Develop a preliminary conceptual model to explain the hydrogeologic function and potential groundwater recharge within the canyon watershed.

Secondary Geologic Issues

Volcanic Hazards

Walnut Canyon National Monument lies south of the San Francisco Volcanic Field, which covers about 4,700 sq km (1,800 sq mi) of northern Arizona (fig. 6). The volcanic field has produced more than 600 volcanoes in its 6 million year history (Priest et al. 2001). Humphreys Peak, Arizona's highest mountain at 3,850 m (12,633 ft), is the only stratovolcano in the field. Stratovolcanoes are cone- shaped volcanoes (e.g., Mt. Rainier), that often rise to a central peak and form by countless eruptions over hundreds of thousands of years.

Most of the volcanoes in the San Francisco Volcanic Field are basaltic cinder cones. In contrast to stratovolcanoes, cinder cones are usually smaller, less than 300 m (1,000 ft) high, and form relatively quickly (months to years). The cones form when basaltic lava erupts as an upward spray, or lava fountain, quickly cools and falls to the ground as dark volcanic rock fragments or cinders. Large fragments are volcanic bombs. A cinder cone builds from this accumulated volcanic debris. (Priest et al. 2001).

The youngest cinder cone in the San Francisco Volcanic Field is Sunset Crater, which erupted between approximately 1080 and 1150 A.D. (http://www.volcano. si.edu/world/volcano.cfm?vnum=1209- 02, accessed March 25, 2007).

The San Francisco Volcanic Field is somewhat anomalous in that typically volcanoes are located near tectonic plate boundaries, rather than well within the interior of the North American Plate. Some evidence suggests that a site of localized melting, or "hot spot," is fixed deep within Earth's mantle, and as the North American Plate moves slowly westward over this stationary source of magma, eruptions produce volcanoes that are strung out progressively eastward (Priest 2001).

Other observations note that the vents associated with the Sunset Crater are aligned along the northeast- trending Colorado Lineament, a major fracture zone in the lithosphere (Luedke and Smith 1991), suggesting a possible structural control to the eruptions rather than a stationary hot spot. For at least the last 15 million years, volcanic eruption have migrated to the northeast (Luedke and Smith 1991; Scott 2004).

Although no eruptions have occurred in the last 1,000 years, volcanic activity could continue in the San Francisco Volcanic Field (Luedke and Smith 1991; Priest et al. 2001). However, predicting the next eruption and possible impacts from such an event on Walnut Canyon National Monument is difficult because the average interval between periods of volcanic activity is several thousand years. Based on past patterns, future eruptions are likely to be small and occur in the eastern part of the field. Nevertheless, ash fall from an eruption could have a large but short- term effect on Walnut Canyon National Monument (Priest et al. 2001).

Seismicity

Although a number of normal faults may have been active in the Walnut Creek area during Quaternary time, only the Anderson Mesa fault and the much smaller Marshall Lake fault, which are located south of the monument, display evidence of significant late Quaternary activity. Rockfall, infrastructure damage, and flash flooding are potential hazards that could result from renewed seismic activity in the area.

Flash Floods

Flash flooding in the canyon has been identified as a hazard in Walnut Canyon, especially for monument staff, researchers, and visitors. Intense rainfall events in the Walnut Creek drainage may quickly trigger flash floods from tributary canyons. If either of the upstream dams were to fail catastrophically, flash floods would inundate Walnut Canyon. Both dams are located along the Lake Mary Fault. Disaster planning and education for flash flooding events could be an important safety undertaking for resource management at Walnut Canyon National Monument.

Fossil Theft

Marine life flourished during the Permian Period, and the fossiliferous limestone in the Kaibab Formation reflects this abundance (fig. 7). Gastropods (snails), pelecypods (clams), scaphopods, cephalopods, brachiopods, trilobites, worm tubes, and shark's teeth in the limestone characterize the marine environment at the time. The fossils can add a significant, visual element to the interpretation of the geologic history of the monument (Vandiver 1936; Santucci and Santucci 1999).

Fossil molds exposed in the Kaibab Formation along the Island Trail to the cliff houses are mostly hollow, plum-sized pits left when groundwater dissolved the fossilized shells. The invertebrate fossils within the Kaibab Formation have little market value as they are small, and often fragments of shells. Also, they are not easily removed from the hard limestone.

Paleontological resources are believed to receive adequate protection by Walnut Canyon staff (NPS 2003). Visitors are allowed only on the 1.4- km (0.9- mi) Island Trail and the Rim Trail limiting access to invertebrate fossils in the Kaibab Formation. Federal law prohibits fossil collecting in units of the National Park System without a research permit regulations at 36 CFR § 2.1 (a) (iii). The monument has documented a few incidents of illegal removal of fossils. Although the theft of marine fossils does not seem to be a serious management problem at this time it is essential that resource management continue to protect this non- renewable resource (NPS 2003; Paul Whitefield, NPS Natural Resource Specialist, written communication, March 29, 2007).

Potential Aquifer Contamination

As discussed above, two principal aquifers underlie Walnut Canyon National Monument (Bills et al. 2000; Thomas 2003). The upper is a local shallow aquifer perched in the Kaibab Formation and the upper part of the Coconino Sandstone. Local precipitation and runoff recharge this aquifer and it discharges water to several springs and seeps near the bottom of Walnut Canyon.

The second principal aquifer is the regional Coconino Aquifer. The Coconino Aquifer is the source of water for most uses in the Flagstaff and Walnut Canyon areas. In the vicinity of Walnut Canyon, depth to the water table is about 457 m (1,500 ft) below the land surface (Bills et al. 2000). Regional groundwater flow is to the northeast (Appel and Bills 1980).

The well at monument headquarters extracts groundwater from the Coconino Aquifer from a depth of 612 m (2,007 ft). Risk of contamination in the Coconino Aquifer is low due to the depth to groundwater, slow groundwater movement, and the natural attenuation of contaminants in the aquifer (NPS 2003; Thomas 2003). Under current levels of extraction within the watershed, there also is little threat of aquifer depletion (NPS 2003).

The primary threats to the water quality in Walnut Canyon are from grazing sheep and cattle on the south side of the canyon and from facilities, such as maintenance shops and sewage lagoons (Thomas 2003). Water resources vulnerable to contamination from these sources include the ephemeral streams, perched groundwater lenses, and the local shallow aquifer. Future impacts to both the regional and local aquifer, however, may come from residential or commercial development of the Walnut Canyon watershed (NPS 2003; Thomas 2003). The city of Flagstaff annexed all the lands to the north and west boundary of Walnut Canyon National Monument. Annexation includes a relatively large area contiguous to the canyon rim and tributary canyons west of the monument. Urban development of these areas could significantly increase non- point source pollution, such as storm sewer runoff, vehicular residue (oil, grease, battery acid and fluids,) fertilizers, herbicides, and pesticides.

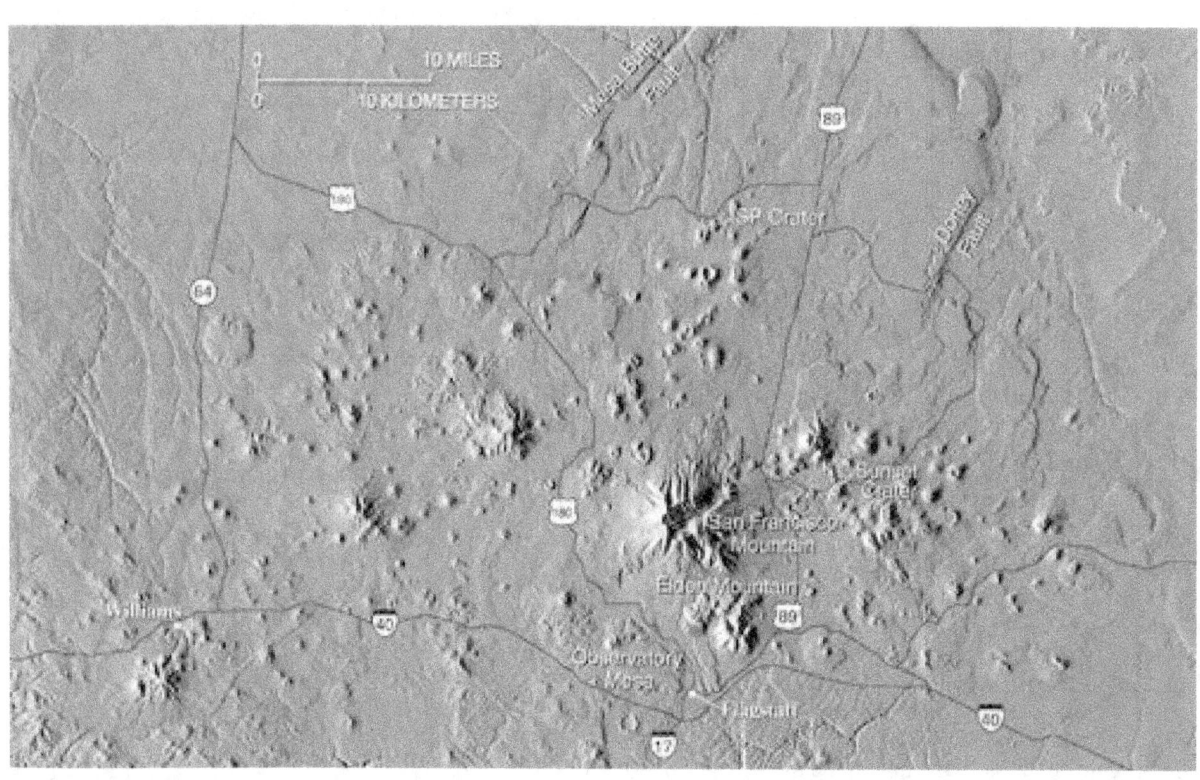

Figure 6. San Francisco Volcanic Field. Many of the more than 600 vents, which have erupted in the area during the past 6 million years, can be seen on this digital elevation model (DEM). Lava flows are flat lobate features near vents. The northeast-trending Mesa Butte Fault and Doney Fault are also labeled. Flagstaff lies at the south-central edge of the volcanic field. Picture is from Priest and others (2001), available at http://geopubs.wr.usgs.gov/fact-sheet/fs017-01/, (Accessed March 2007).

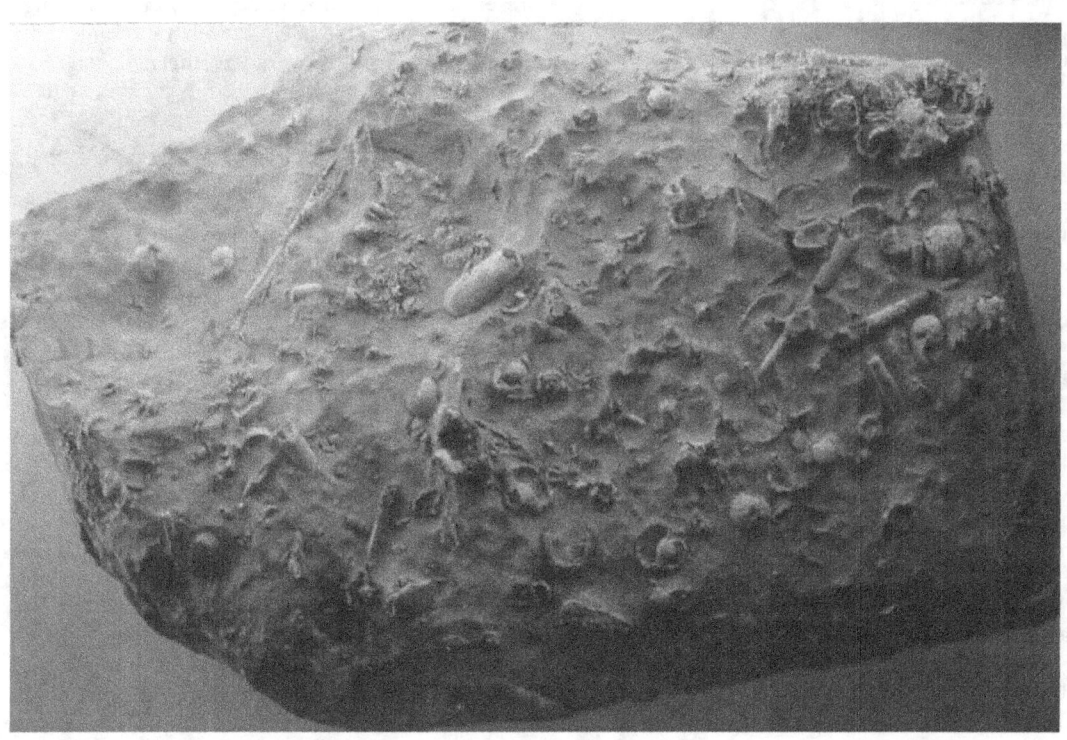

Figure 7. Representative sample of the fossiliferous limestone in the Kaibab Formation. Long tapered shells are scaphopods; circular shell fragments are brachiopod valves. This sample is from the Coconino Plateau, but not specifically from Walnut Canyon National Monument. Photo is courtesy of Northern Arizona University and found at http://oak.ucc.nau.edu/llc7/Photo%20Albums/Geology/ slides/Kaibab%20Limestone %20Marine%20Fossils.html, (Accessed March 2007).

Geologic Features and Processes

This section provides descriptions of the most prominent and distinctive geologic features and processes in Walnut Canyon National Monument.

Geologic features at Walnut Canyon National Monument range in scale from fossil fragments embedded in limestone to faulting visible from satellite imagery. Processes that formed these features are equally diverse, including aeolian processes that formed ancient sand dunes, regional tectonic uplift, and erosion that carved Walnut Canyon.

Geomorphic Features

Walnut Canyon is the dominant geologic feature in Walnut Canyon National Monument (fig. 8). Downcutting of Walnut Canyon by Walnut Creek has occurred over the last five million years, carving a steep-walled canyon averaging about 350 feet (107 m) deep (Chronic 1983; http://3dparks.wr.usgs.gov/walnutcanyon/html/wc1640.htm, accessed March 2007). Walnut Creek incised into bedrock analogous to the Colorado River at the Grand Canyon – downcutting accelerated by regional uplift. Uplift of the Colorado Plateau began about 65 Ma at the beginning of the Tertiary Period, and periods of uplift followed into the late Tertiary. Continued uplift of the Colorado Plateau forced Walnut Creek to cut into the underlying bedrock while maintaining its original meander pattern (Rowlands et al. 1995). A stream that inherits its channel from a previous erosion cycle cuts into bedrock by overprinting the pre- existing channel morphology becoming entrenched (fig. 8).

Today, Walnut Creek is an underfit stream or a stream that appears too small to have eroded the canyon in which it flows. However, the flow in Walnut Creek was probably much greater during the wetter Pleistocene Epoch more than 10,000 years ago when precipitation and runoff on the Coconino Plateau were much higher than today (Rowlands et al. 1995).

Sharp, angular turns in Walnut Creek correspond with joint orientations in the walls of the canyon indicating a marked influence of pre- existing geologic structures on the geomorphology of the canyon. Deformation associated with large, north- south trending regional faults may have influenced joint orientations in Walnut Canyon (fig. 3) (Henkle 1976; Rowlands 1995).

Geomorphic processes have reworked coarse- grained colluvium and eroded fine- grained sand from the Coconino Sandstone into a variety of depositional types. Deposits include upland terrace alluvium, coarse channel and channel bar deposits, dunes, and scour holes, establishing distinctive vegetation patterns based on sediment and water availability (Rowlands et al. 1995). For example, Douglas fir, Gambel oak, and snowberry dragon sage prefer upland terrace deposits, whereas Arizona rose, New Mexico locust, and red osier dogwood thrive in streambed and channel bar deposits.

Sedimentary Features

The buff- colored Coconino Sandstone forms the walls of the steep lower portion of Walnut Canyon. Sweeping cross- beds of aeolian sandstone are the primary sedimentary features in this unit (fig. 9). Cross- bedding preserves migrating foreset dunes that formed roughly 275- 280 Ma near an ancient Permian shoreline (Peterson 1980). The dune field covered northern Arizona, southern Utah, and northwestern New Mexico at a time when the landscape and climate were similar to today's Sahara desert. Other sedimentary features found in the Coconino Sandstone include raindrop impressions, wind ripple marks, and sand avalanches that once slid off the over- steepened front of a migrating dune.

The fossiliferous marine limestone of the Kaibab Formation contrasts with the underlying, aeolian cross-bedded Coconino Sandstone (fig. 9). The Kaibab Formation outcrops in the cliffs of the upper third of Walnut Canyon. Thick, erosion- resistant, gray limestone ledges separate slopes of soft, thinly interlayered, silty limestone or limy sandstone (fig. 4). Limestone in the Kaibab indicates an ancient marine regression into the region. During this time, sea level fluctuated cyclically. When sea level rose, shallow, open marine conditions prevailed supporting a diverse marine ecosystem that included brachiopods, sponges, and other marine invertebrates. When sea level fell, faunal diversity decreased and near- shore limy sand and silt accumulated. These contrasting depositional environments became the alternating limestone ledges and carbonate sandstone slopes exposed in Walnut Canyon.

Chert nodules are abundant in some of the limestone layers. These nodules formed from sponge spicules, skeletal elements of sponges composed of minute needles of silica. When the sponges died, these siliceous spicules accumulated on the ocean floor, and with subsequent burial and pressure from overlying sediment, the silica formed nodules of chert. Chert (flint) formed from spicules is hard and dense and was widely used for various tools and spear points by early Native Americans throughout the western United States. However, there is no evidence that the Sinagua of Walnut Canyon used chert. This could be due to vandalism and theft of the Sinagua cultural resources at Walnut Canyon prior to protection by the federal government.

Tectonic Deformation

Sedimentary features, such as sand dunes, result from processes that focus on individual grains or fragments of material whereas tectonic features form through processes that deform the crust and lithosphere. Plate tectonic processes involve plates separating from each other along continental and oceanic rifts, sliding past each other along transverse margins, and colliding into each other forming mountain chains and subduction zones (fig. 10). As plates collide, one plate may subduct beneath the other and create a deep trench in which vast amounts of sediments accumulate. These sediments may combine with bits of oceanic crust and small landmasses such as islands and island arcs to form an accretionary wedge between the two plates. If this wedge accretes to the edge of the overriding plate, the continent grows in size.

Throughout the middle Paleozoic Era and into the Mesozoic Era, western North America had been an active collisional margin where dense oceanic crust subducted beneath the lighter continental crust of the North America lithospheric plate. Compressive forces produced thrust faulting and large- scale folding of originally horizontal sedimentary geologic units. Remnants of these thrust faults and folds appear in mountain ranges west of the Colorado Plateau province.

About 20 Ma subduction off the southwestern coast of North America ceased and the lithospheric plates began to slide past one another, generating strike- slip faulting culminating in the San Andreas fault system of California (Pallister et al. 1997). Strike- slip faulting and high heat flow beneath the southwestern region of the United States resulted in crustal extension. Large crustal blocks dropped down along high- angle normal faults, creating grabens (structural basins) adjacent to relatively uplifted blocks (horsts) forming mountain ranges. This type of regional faulting produced the characteristic topography of the Basin- and- Range physiographic province of the western United States.

The Colorado Plateau remained relatively stable throughout this tectonic deformation to the west. The crustal extension that affected parts of Utah, Nevada, Arizona, and New Mexico did not significantly deform the interior of the Colorado Plateau. However, normal faulting did occur along the margins of the province.

The Anderson Mesa fault is a typical structure generated by Basin- and- Range extensional faulting. This fault is the most prominent feature in the rectilinear pattern of lineaments that crisscross the Coconino Plateau (fig. 3).

The lineaments shown on figure 3 are fractures and normal faults controlled by deep- seated, Precambrian crustal structures that have been periodically reactivated throughout geologic time. Located south of Walnut Canyon National Monument, the Anderson Mesa fault follows a trend oriented approximately 65 degrees northwest along Upper Lake Mary and Lower Lake Mary before striking due north along the north- south trending part of Walnut Canyon (Rowlands et al. 1995).

Topographic displacement along the Anderson Mesa fault is 60 m (197 ft) (Rowlands et al. 1995). Many smaller faults that postdate the Anderson Mesa fault strike parallel to the main fault and delineate the graben later forming Upper and Lower Lake Mary (fig. 3) (Rowlands et al. 1995).

Numerous joints and fractures occur in Walnut Canyon and may have influenced the drainage pattern of Walnut Creek (Rowlands et al. 1995). North- south joint orientations probably reflect the trends of larger faults in the region. Joints and fractures affect the hydrogeologic system of the area. The highly fractured rocks locally transmit from 10 to 50 times as much groundwater as do adjacent, unfractured rocks of the same unit.

Fossils

The brachiopod *Dictyoclostus* is the most common fossil exposed along the Island Trail. Other fossils include spiral impressions of snails and molds of small clams (Chronic 1983). Several molds of brachiopod fossils are scattered along the back wall of the cliff dwellings.

Invertebrate fossils from the Kaibab Formation in Walnut Canyon National Monument and the surrounding area include bryozoans, mollusks, brachiopods, trilobites, sponges, echinoderms, and worm tubes (table 1) (Santucci and Santucci 1999). Teeth from a variety of sharks appear in the Kaibab including *Sandalodus*, *Deltodus*, *Symmorium*, *Petalodus*, and *Orrodus* and phyllodont tooth plates.

The dune deposits of the underlying Coconino Sandstone yield fewer fossils than the marine limestone in the Kaibab Formation. Low diversity vertebrate and invertebrate trace fossils are reported from within the Coconino Sandstone, but not from Walnut Canyon National Monument (Santucci and Santucci 1999; Middleton et al. 2003). Trace fossils in the Coconino include trails, tracks, burrows, borings, tubes, tunnels or other impressions in the sediments caused by animal activity.

Table 1. Invertebrate fossils from the Kaibab Formation in Walnut Canyon NM area

Phylum	Class	Genus sp./other
Mollusca	Gastropoda	*Baylea* sp
		Bellerophon deflectus
		Euomphalus sp
		Euphemites sp
		Goniasma sp
		Murchisonia sp
		Naticopsis sp
		Pennotrochus arizonensis
		Soleniscus sp
		Busyconids
	Pelecypoda	*Allorisma* sp
		Astarella sp
		Aviculopecten kaibabensis
		Dozierella sp
		Edmondia sp
		Gramatodon politus
		Janeia sp
		Kaibabella curvilinata
		Myalina sp
		Myalinella adunca
		Nuculana sp
		Nuculopsis sp
		Palaeonucula levatiformis
		Parallelodon sp
		Permophorous albequus
		Pleurophorus albequus
		Schizodus texanus
		Solemya sp
		Solenomorpha sp
	Scaphalopoda	*Plagioglypta canna*
	Cephalopoda	*Aulometacoceras* sp
		Metacoceras unklesbayi
		Stearoceras sp
		Tainoceras sp
Brachiopoda		*Chonetes* sp
		Composita arizonica
		Dictyoclostus sp
		Marginifera sp
		Peniculauris bassi
		Quadrochonetes kaibabensis
		Rugatia paraindica
Arthropoda	Trilobita	*Anisopyge* sp
		Ditomopyge sp
Annelida		Worm tubes
Bryozoa		Fragments

Figure 8. Walnut Canyon, Walnut Canyon National Monument. The meander pattern of the canyon reflects the entrenched meander pattern of Walnut Creek. Photo courtesy of the U.S. Geologic Survey, http://3dparks.wr.usgs.gov/walnutcanyon/html/wc1640.htm, (Accessed March 2007).

Figure 9. Cross-bedded Coconino Sandstone, Walnut Canyon National Monument. Overlapping sets of cross-beds denote migrating sand dunes similar to active processes today in modern dune fields. Photo courtesy of http://geoweb.tamu.edu/RGallery/zion2003/six/6i.html, (Accessed March 2007).

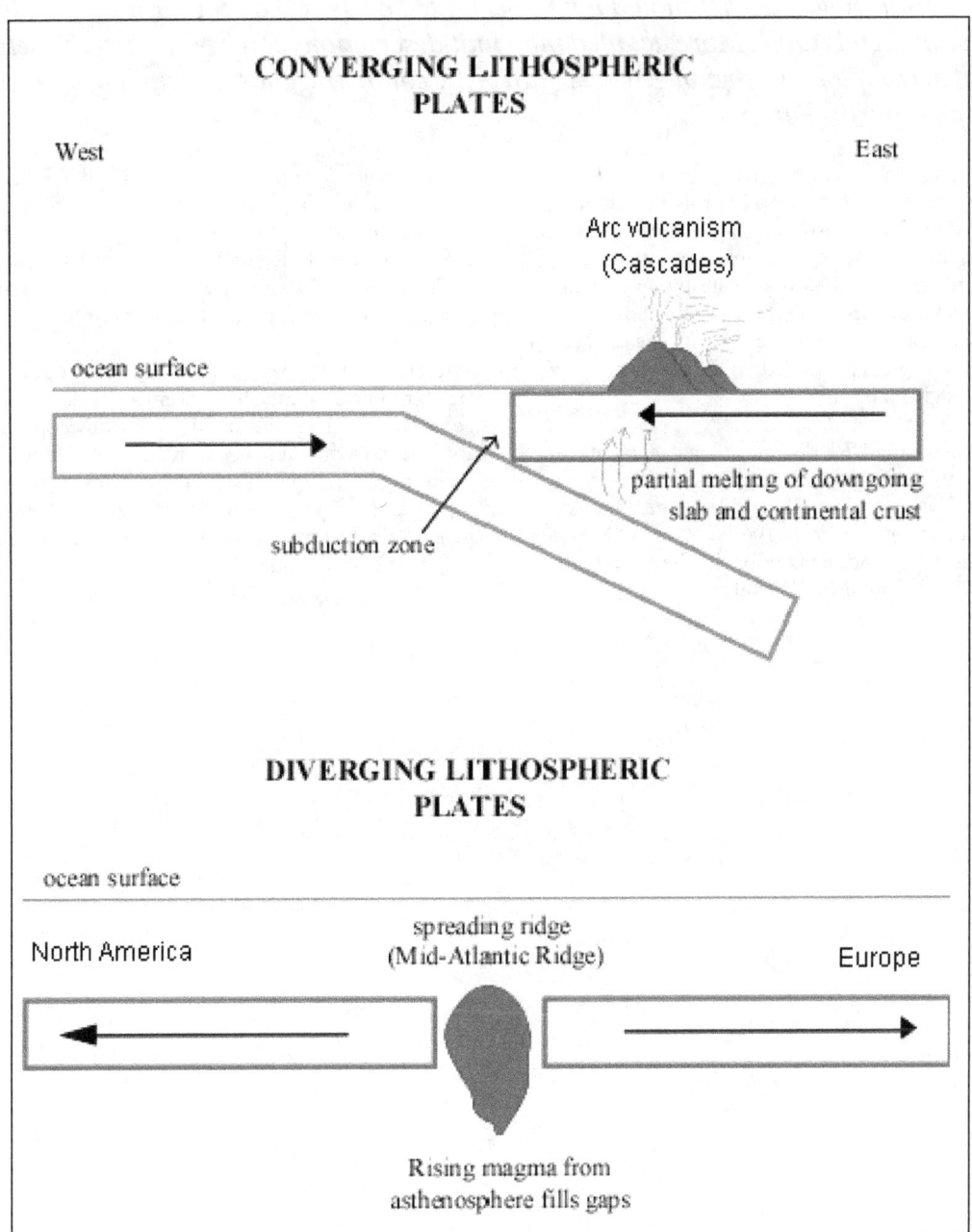

Figure 10. Schematic of converging and diverging lithospheric plates according to plate tectonic theory.

Map Unit Properties

This section identifies characteristics of map units that appear on the Geologic Resource Evaluation digital geologic map of Walnut Canyon National Monument. The accompanying table is highly generalized and is provided for background purposes only. Ground- disturbing activities should not be permitted or denied on the basis of information in this table. More detailed map unit descriptions can be found in the help files that accompany the digital geologic map or by contacting the National Park Service Geologic Resources Division.

The following Map Unit Properties Table identifies specific properties of the different geologic map units that may be useful for resource management decision making. Geologic features and processes often occur in or can be restricted to a particular stratigraphic unit (group, formation, or member). This table ties together the geologic features and processes with the properties of the geologic units presented on the accompanying digital geologic map.

Source data for the GRE digital geologic map are from:

Raucci, J., Blythe, N., Ort, M., and Manone, M. 2003. *Geologic Map of the Greater Walnut Canyon National Monument Area*. Scale 1:12,000. Northern Arizona University. Unpublished digital map.

For a detailed list of references used in the development of this source map please refer to the help file that accompanies the digital geologic map. Digital geologic map data are included on the attached CD and are also available on the Web (http://www.nature.nps.gov/geology/inventory/gre_publications.cfm).

The Map Unit Properties Table presents the stratigraphic column and an itemized list of features per geologic unit. The table includes several properties specific to each unit in the stratigraphic column including age, map unit symbol, unit description, topographic expression of the unit, erosion resistance, paleontologic and cultural resources, hazards, and a miscellaneous column.

Map Unit Properties Table

Age	Map Unit (symbol)	Unit Description	Topographic Expression	Erosion Resistance	Paleontological Resources	Cultural Resources	Hazards	Other
QUATERNARY	Alluvium (Qal)	Unconsolidated fluvial deposits; thickness to 75 ft (23 m)	Canyon bottom	Low	None	None documented	None	Locally perched water table
QUATERNARY	Lacustrine (Ql)	Fine-grained lake deposits	Canyon bottom	Low				Limited exposures
QUATERNARY	Colluvial (Qc)	Unconsolidated deposits at the base of the canyon walls; maximum thickness 148+ feet (45+ m)	Base of canyon walls	High				Limited exposures
QUATERNARY	Basalt colluvium (Qbc)	Unconsolidated basalt deposits at the base of the canyon walls	Base of canyon walls	High				Limited exposures
QUATERNARY	Basalt (Qb)	Basalt of Lower Lake Mary flow; not in monument	NA	NA	NA	NA	NA	Not exposed in monument
TERTIARY	Volcanic rocks (Tb)	Basalt from the Anderson Mesa flow; lava flows are about 125 ft (38 m) thick within the Lake Mary Graben & are covered by Quaternary alluvium; not in monument.	Caps Anderson Mesa, south of WACA	NA	NA	NA	NA	Not exposed in monument
LOWER TRIASSIC	Moenkopi Fm (TRm)	Reddish-brown mudstone, siltstone, & sandstone. Mostly eroded from area; present only in patchy outcrops along the upthrown side of the Anderson Mesa fault, in the Marshall Lake Graben, & in narrow grabens in Walnut Canyon; thickness from 0-394 ft (0-120 m)	Limited exposures; present in low topographic areas	Siltstone & mudstone is less resistant to erosion than the sandstone layers	Amphibian & reptile tracks found to the north in Wupatki National Monument	None documented	None documented	Limited exposures
LOWER PERMIAN	Kaibab Fm (Pkf)	Gray, silty dolomite; sandy limestone, fossiliferous & cherty limestone; 364 ft (111 m) thick	Caprock of canyon; ledges of dolomite & limestone separated by slopes or recesses of silty limestone or limy sandstone	Resistant dolomitic limestone ledges; alcoves eroded into less resistant sandy limestone interlayers	Abundant marine invertebrate fossils: gastropods, pelecypods, cephalopods, brachiopods, scaphopods, trilobites, sponges, echinoderms, worm tubes; variety of shark's teeth	Cliff dwellings built in less resistant, recessive layers between resistant limestone ledges	Rockfall potential exists where Kaibab may collapse into underlying, less resistant layers	Vertical fractures parallel to canyon; infrastructure & park buildings developed on Kaibab caprock
LOWER PERMIAN	Coconino Sandstone (Pc)	Light colored, fine-grained, well-sorted, rounded quartz sandstone, highly cross-stratified, exposed in canyon walls below Kaibab Formation; includes the overlying cross-bedded sandstone of the Toroweap Fm; 738 ft (225 m) thick	Forms steep cliffs in lower third of Walnut Canyon	Resistant to erosion but permeable to ground water	No vertebrate or invertebrate trace fossils in monument; three trace fossil species of *Chelichnus* (caseid-like reptile tracks) found outside of monument	None documented	Potential rockfall	Aeolian sandstone aquifer

Geologic History

This section highlights the map units (i.e., rocks and unconsolidated deposits) that occur in Walnut Canyon National Monument and puts them in a geologic context in terms of the environment in which they were deposited and the timing of geologic events that created the present landscape.

The oldest rocks exposed in Walnut Canyon National Monument are Upper Paleozoic (Permian), about 275 million years old (fig. 11). The geologic history of the southwestern United States is millions of years older. In Grand Canyon National Park to the north, the Elves Chasm pluton outcrops and is the oldest rock unit found in the southwestern United States at 1,840 million years old. (Pallister et al. 1997; Karlstrom et al., 2003).

During the Precambrian, the Southwest may have looked like the western Pacific today with numerous volcanic belts separated by seas (Hoffman 1989; Pallister et al. 1997). The southwestern coastline of North America paralleled the present border of Wyoming and Colorado. As crustal plates collided, volcanic belts, or island arcs developed and accreted terrane to the margins of North America in the process of continental growth. Through this process of accretion, most of Arizona was added to the North American continent by 1.4 billion years ago.

In Arizona a major unconformity, representing approximately 800 million years of missing geologic history, separates the Precambrian units from Cambrian- age units (fig. 11). Cambrian rocks in Arizona record a major advance of the sea into the area about 520 Ma. Throughout the Paleozoic Era, epicontinental seas advanced (transgressed) and retreated (regressed) depositing thick layers of limestone and sandstone on the sea floor.

Permian Period

Towards the end of the Paleozoic, landmasses were becoming tectonically sutured together to form a "supercontinent" called Pangaea. Approximately 275 Ma the Permian equator on the western margin of Pangaea was oriented southwest- northeast through modern Wyoming and eastern Utah (Biek et al. 2000; Morris et al. 2000). A dry, high atmospheric pressure climatic belt prevailed in this western part of Pangaea and resulted in restricted- marine evaporitic conditions over much of southwestern North America (Peterson 1980).

The sweeping high- angle, cross- stratification in the Coconino Sandstone preserves ancient sand dunes that were part of a very extensive, Sahara- like aeolian dune field, called an erg, which extended from Arizona to Montana (fig. 12) (McCormack 1989; Middleton et al. 2003). The Coconino Sandstone is composed of fine-grained, well- sorted, rounded quartz grains and is correlative to the Weber Sandstone in Utah and the Tensleep Sandstone in Wyoming and Montana.

Some of the beds of cross- stratification in the Coconino Sandstone are up to 20 m (66 ft) thick. Vertebrate and invertebrate tracks and trails in the sandstone suggest animals traversed the loose dune sand (Middleton et al. 2003). These sediments and trace fossils record the advance and passage of a major aeolian sand sea.

In northern Arizona the Coconino Sandstone is overlain by, or interlayered with, the Permian Toroweap Formation. In the Walnut Canyon National Monument area, the Toroweap consists of cross- bedded aeolian sandstone that is indistinguishable from the Coconino Sandstone. The aeolian sandstone of the Coconino grades eastward into near- shore marine sandstone beds of the Glorieta Sandstone in western New Mexico. To the south, the Coconino Sandstone is either interbedded with reddish- brown erg- margin sandstones, siltstones, gypsum (Schnebly Hill Formation) and tidal- flat deposits (Toroweap Formation), or it is sharply overlain by the Kaibab Formation. The Toroweap and the Kaibab Formation reflect a transgressive episode in which the marine environment to the west inundated the Coconino sand dune field covering the area with marine sediments.

The Middle Permian Kaibab Formation is the youngest Paleozoic rock unit on the southern Colorado Plateau and preserves evidence of an ancient seaway that spread over most of northern Arizona about 260 million years ago (fig. 13) (Hopkins and Thompson, 2003). At this time, the last of the Paleozoic epicontinental seas transgressed into northern Arizona. The subtidal, shallow marine environments of the Kaibab formed a mixed carbonate-clastic ramp (Hopkins and Thompson, 2003).

Invertebrate fossils in the Kaibab Formation at Walnut Canyon National Monument once lived in a regressive shallow marine environment (Santucci and Santucci 1999). The pelecypod *Schizodus* usually lived in shallow hypersaline environments. The fossil assemblage in table 1 is characteristic of fauna of nearshore brackish environments. This regressive shallow marine interpretation is supported by the absence of corals in the assemblage. Permian corals, like modern corals, preferred open, oxygenated marine environments with good water circulation.

The Kaibab Formation on the Coconino Plateau is composed of a variety of lithologic types. The interbedded carbonate and clastic sediments of the Kaibab record a complex depositional history. The repetitive and cyclic nature of these deposits documents repeated depositional shifts of near- shore and shallow marine depositional environments during pulsed transgressions and regressions of the epicontinental sea into the region (Hopkins and Thompson 2003).

The episodic transgressions and regressions were a result of the tectonic activity at the margins of the North American continent as the global landmasses were coming together to form Pangaea. During the Permian Period, the western margin of Pangaea continued to undergo compression as lithospheric plates collided (Silberling and Roberts 1962). The peaks of the Uncompahgre Mountains were formed in western Colorado from compressional stresses resulting from the collision of South American with the southern edge of North America.

The close of the Permian brought the third, and most extensive, major mass extinction of geologic time (fig. 13). Although not as widely known as the extinction event at the end of the Mesozoic Era that exterminated the dinosaurs, the Permian extinction event eliminated approximately 96% of all species (Raup 1991).

Triassic Period

During the Triassic Period (251- 200 Ma), the supercontinent Pangaea reached its greatest size. All the continents had come together to form a single landmass that was centered on the equator (Dubiel, 1994). On the western margin, volcanoes erupted from the sea and formed a north- south trending arc of islands along the border of what is now California and Nevada (fig. 14) (Christiansen et al. 1994; Dubiel 1994; Lawton 1994).

A shallow sea stretched from eastern Utah to eastern Nevada over a beveled continental shelf in the Early Triassic (fig. 14). The depositional environments in the Lower Triassic Moenkopi Formation range from offshore marine to continental alluvial fan and include fluvial, mudflat, sabkha, and shallow marine sediments (Stewart et al. 1972; Dubiel 1994). Fossilized plants and animals in the Moenkopi Formation suggest a climate shift from the arid, desert conditions at the end of the Permian to a warm tropical setting that may have experienced monsoonal, wet- dry conditions in this region of North America (Stewart et al. 1972; Dubiel 1994).

Most of the Moenkopi Formation has been eroded from the upper reaches of the Walnut Canyon area. Limited exposures of mudstones and thinly bedded sandstones preserve shallow marine depositional environments such as tidal flats. Lower Triassic strata throughout the western U.S. indicate that at least three major transgressive- regressive cycles occurred in the Early Triassic. The presence of an ammonoid fossil in the lower Moenkopi Formation, discovered at Wupatki National Monument, indicates that an incursion of a shallow sea into this region of northern Arizona took place during one of those cycles. (McCormack 1989).

The Missing Record

By the end of the Mesozoic Era, Pangaea was broken apart into roughly the continents present today. In Arizona, about 1.6 km (1 mi) of terrestrial and marine rock layers covered the Kaibab Formation (Billingsley 1989; Morales 2003). Uplift of the southwestern Colorado Plateau during the Tertiary, however, initiated a major episode of erosion that stripped away the Mesozoic rocks from the Walnut Canyon region (Lucchitta 2003). Tertiary and Pleistocene rocks and sediments also are missing from the region – either never deposited, or removed by erosion. In Walnut Canyon National Monument, the unconformity between the Moenkopi Formation and the first Quaternary deposits spans approximately 245 million years.

During the Mesozoic Era, a volcanic island arc formed off the coast of western North America. Subduction zones associated with plate collision underlay the southern part of Arizona, south of the Walnut Canyon region (Pallister et al. 1997). Volcanoes typically form over subduction zones as the subducting plate melts creating a magma source.

A tectonic regime change in the Early Cretaceous from compression to extension initiated rifting in the northwest- southeast trending Bisbee Basin of southeastern Arizona (Elder and Kirkland 1994; Dickinson and Lawton 2001; Haenggi and Muehlberger 2005). Rifting tilted the Mogollon slope towards the northeast and opened a series of local pull- apart basins in southern Arizona (Elder and Kirkland 1994; Anderson and Nourse 2005). Streams on the Mogollon flowed to the northeast, similar to Walnut Creek. Northeast flowing streams emptied into the last epicontinental sea that inundated the North American continent (fig. 15). This interior seaway extended from the Gulf of Mexico to the Arctic Ocean and from Nebraska to central Nevada.

At the close of the Mesozoic, about 65 Ma, another burst of volcanic activity and faulting in southeastern Arizona resulted from the Laramide Orogeny (about 75- 35 Ma). This episode of tectonic compression and mountain building formed the modern Rocky Mountains and emplaced most of the ores of copper, silver, and gold in the southwestern United States (Pallister et al. 1997). The Laramide Orogeny caused uplift of the southwestern Colorado Plateau and subsequent erosion of most of the Mesozoic strata from the Walnut Canyon area. North- flowing, sediment- choked streams dominated the landscape and covered parts of northern Arizona with 100 to 200 m (330 to 660 ft) of gravelly sediments.

The Laramide Orogeny uplifted the Colorado Plateau, reactivated Precambrian faults in a reverse sense, and horizontally shortened the western margin of North America across north- south trending thrust faults (Marshak et al. 2000; Billingsley and Wellmeyer 2002; Huntoon 2003). On the Colorado Plateau, east- dipping monoclines formed in Paleozoic and Mesozoic strata and overlie deep- seated, west- dipping reverse faults.

Intervening blocks between monoclines gently warped into broad, north- trending arches and basins.

About 45 Ma (Eocene), plate movement along the west coast subduction zone slowed, resulting in a cessation of deformation in the Walnut Canyon area (Dickinson 1981; Huntoon 2003). Subduction remained active in the southwestern United States and volcanism continued in southern Arizona during early to middle Tertiary. The Santa Catalina Mountains of southern Arizona contain at least 12 plutons emplaced in three intrusive episodes: 1) 60- 75 Ma (Latest Cretaceous to Paleocene), 2) 44- 50 Ma (Eocene), and 3) 25- 29 Ma (Oligocene) (Anderson 1988).

Miocene to Recent

Subduction off the southwestern coast of North America ceased about 20 Ma and the relative motion of the plates changed from compressional to transverse, initiating the strike- slip San Andreas fault system and extension of the crust that would lead to Basin- and- Range normal faulting. During the Miocene and Pliocene, the Colorado Plateau uplifted as much as 3- 4 km (1.8- 2.5 mi) (Oldow et al. 1989).

The San Francisco volcanic field, north of Walnut Canyon National Monument, was the major volcanic center on the southwest margin of the Colorado Plateau (Luedke and Smith 1991). Locally, the Anderson Mesa basalt was extruded during the Pliocene. Volcanic activity was almost continuous during the late Cenozoic, particularly in the Pliocene and Pleistocene. Volcanic eruptions in the San Francisco volcanic field continued

into the Holocene. The most recent eruptive activity took place about 1,000 years ago, forming Sunset Crater, Arizona's youngest volcano (Priest et al. 2001).

Walnut Creek is a tributary to the Little Colorado River, which flows into the Colorado River. The Colorado River began incising the Grand Canyon about 5 Ma (Spencer et al. 2001; Lucchitta 2003) and its tributaries did the same. Radiometric ages of volcanic rocks and geomorphic features along the canyon indicate that by 3.8 Ma, the Colorado River was essentially at its present grade in the upper Lake Mead area, and by 1 Ma, it was at its present grade in the western Grand Canyon (Lucchitta and Jeanne 2001; Hamblin 2003; Lucchitta 2003).

The alluvial, colluvial, and lake deposits in Walnut Canyon National Monument are the latest chapter in the geologic history of the region. Channel downcutting in the Holocene left alluvial terrace deposits in the canyons. Headward erosion provided additional sediment that was transported and deposited to form channel bars, point bars, and other alluvial deposits. Lake deposits in Walnut Canyon resulted from the impoundment of Walnut Creek by the Santa Fe Dam. Mass wasting processes work to widen canyons on the Colorado Plateau and generate colluvium in the form of talus slopes at the base of the cliffs. Visitors to Walnut Canyon National Monument are allowed a glimpse into the erosion and depositional processes that were ongoing throughout geologic history and that continue to shape the present landscapes.

Eon	Era	Period	Epoch	Ma	Life Forms	N. American Tectonics
Phanerozoic (Phaneros = "evident"; zoic = "life")	Cenozoic	Quaternary	Recent, or Holocene	0.01	*Age of Mammals* — Modern humans; Extinction of large mammals and birds	Cascade volcanoes; Worldwide glaciation
			Pleistocene	1.8		
		Tertiary	Pliocene	5.3	Large carnivores; Whales and apes	Uplift of Sierra Nevada; Linking of N. and S. America
			Miocene	23.0		Basin-and-Range extension
			Oligocene	33.9		
			Eocene	55.8	Early primates	Laramide orogeny ends (W)
			Paleocene	65.5		
	Mesozoic	Cretaceous		145.5	*Age of Dinosaurs* — Mass extinction; Placental mammals; Early flowering plants	Laramide orogeny (W); Sevier orogeny (W); Nevadan orogeny (W)
		Jurassic		199.6	First mammals; Mass extinction; Flying reptiles; First dinosaurs	Elko orogeny (W); Breakup of Pangaea begins; Sonoma orogeny (W)
		Triassic		251		
	Paleozoic	Permian		299	*Age of Amphibians* — Mass extinction; Coal-forming forests diminish	Supercontinent Pangaea intact; Ouachita orogeny (S); Alleghenian (Appalachian) orogeny (E); Ancestral Rocky Mts. (W)
		Pennsylvanian		318.1	Coal-forming swamps; Sharks abundant; Variety of insects	
		Mississippian		359.2	First amphibians; First reptiles	Antler orogeny (W)
		Devonian		416	*Fishes* — Mass extinction; First forests (evergreens)	Acadian orogeny (E-NE)
		Silurian		443.7	First land plants; Mass extinction	
		Ordovician		488.3	*Marine Invertebrates* — First primitive fish; Trilobite maximum; Rise of corals	Taconic orogeny (NE)
		Cambrian		542	Early shelled organisms	Avalonian orogeny (NE); Extensive oceans cover most of N. America
Proterozoic ("Early life")		Precambrian		2500	First multicelled organisms; Jellyfish fossil (670 Ma)	Formation of early supercontinent; Grenville orogeny (E); First iron deposits; Abundant carbonate rocks
Archean ("Ancient")				≈3600	Early bacteria and algae	Oldest known Earth rocks (≈3.93 billion years ago)
Hadean ("Beneath the Earth")				4600	Origin of life?	Oldest moon rocks (4-4.6 billion years ago); Earth's crust being formed
					Formation of the Earth	

Figure 11. Geologic time scale; adapted from the U.S. Geological Survey and the International Commission on Stratigraphy. Red lines indicate major unconformities between eras. Included are major events in the history of life on Earth and tectonic events occurring on the North American continent. Absolute ages shown are in millions of years (Ma, or mega-annum).

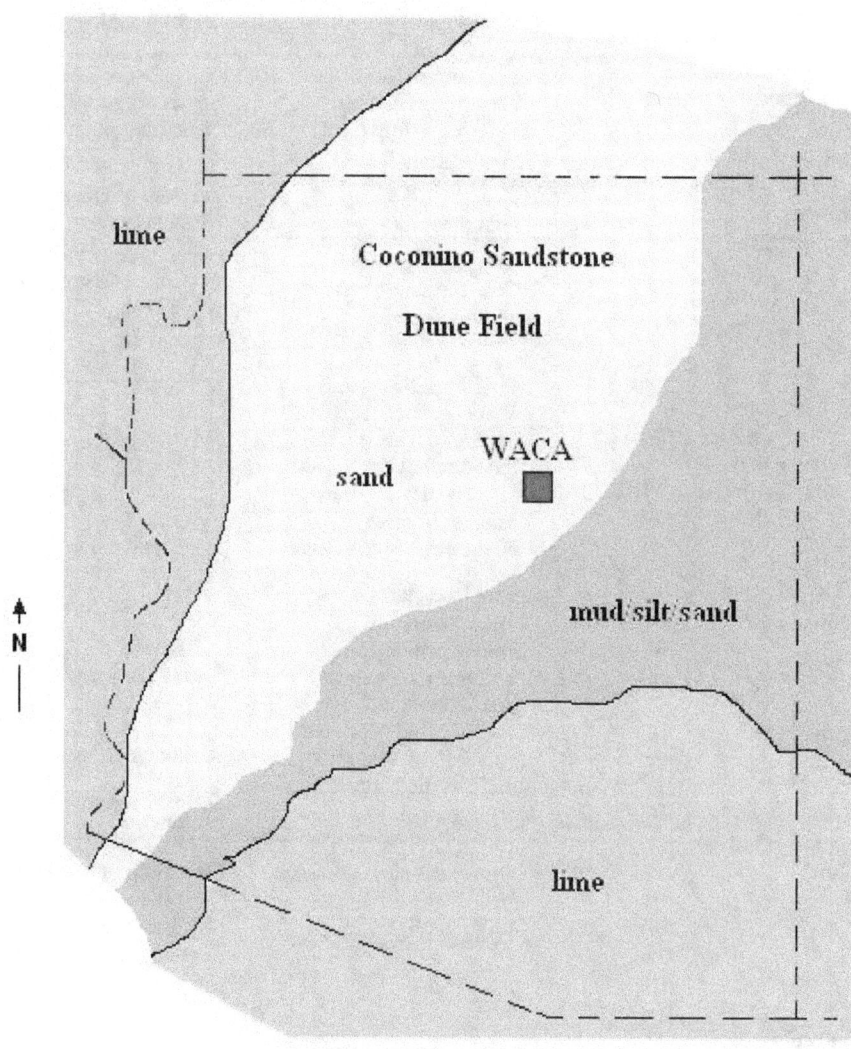

Figure 12. Generalized paleogeographic map showing the approximate distribution of Coconino Sandstone in Arizona during the Permian, approximately 170 Ma. Modified from Middleton and others (2003) and Dr. Ron Blakey, Northern Arizona University, Department of Geology, http://jan.ucc.nau.edu/~rcb7/perpaleo.html, (Accessed March 2007).

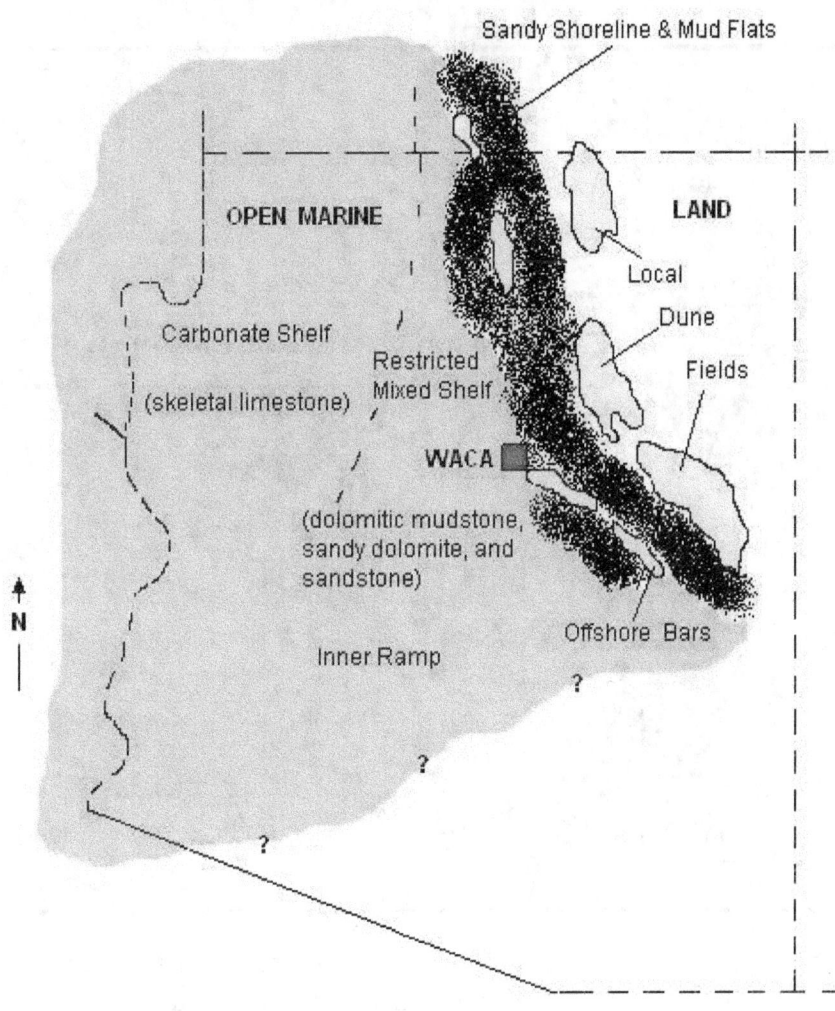

Figure 13. Paleogeographic map of northern Arizona during deposition of the Kaibab Formation. Modified from Hopkins and Thompson (2003).

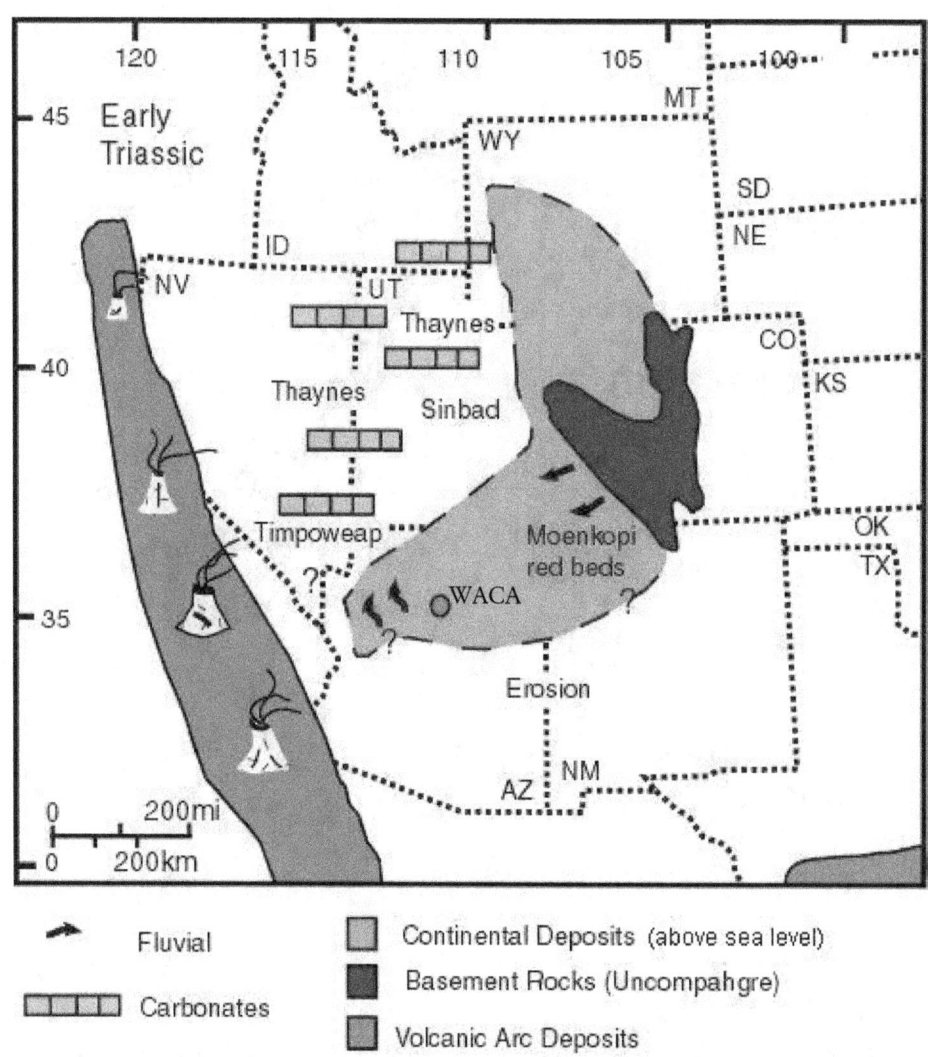

Figure 14. Paleogeographic map of the Early Triassic during deposition of the Moenkopi Formation. Modified from Dubiel (1994).

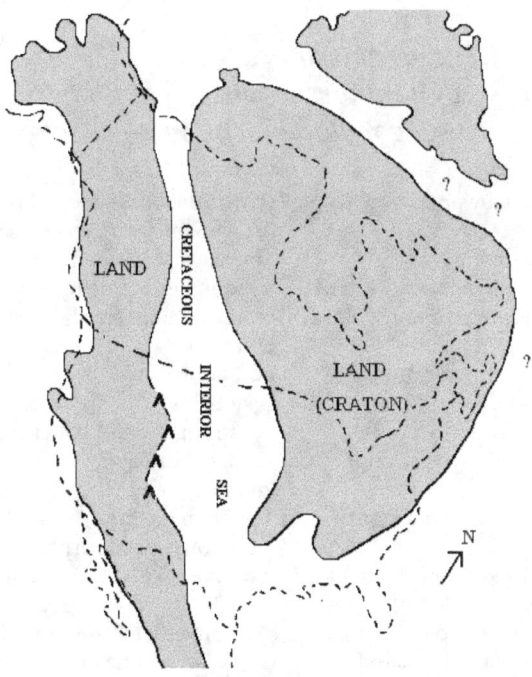

Figure 15A. Late Cretaceous interior seaway. The sea extended from the Gulf of Mexico to the Arctic Ocean. Modified from Rice and Shurr, (1983).

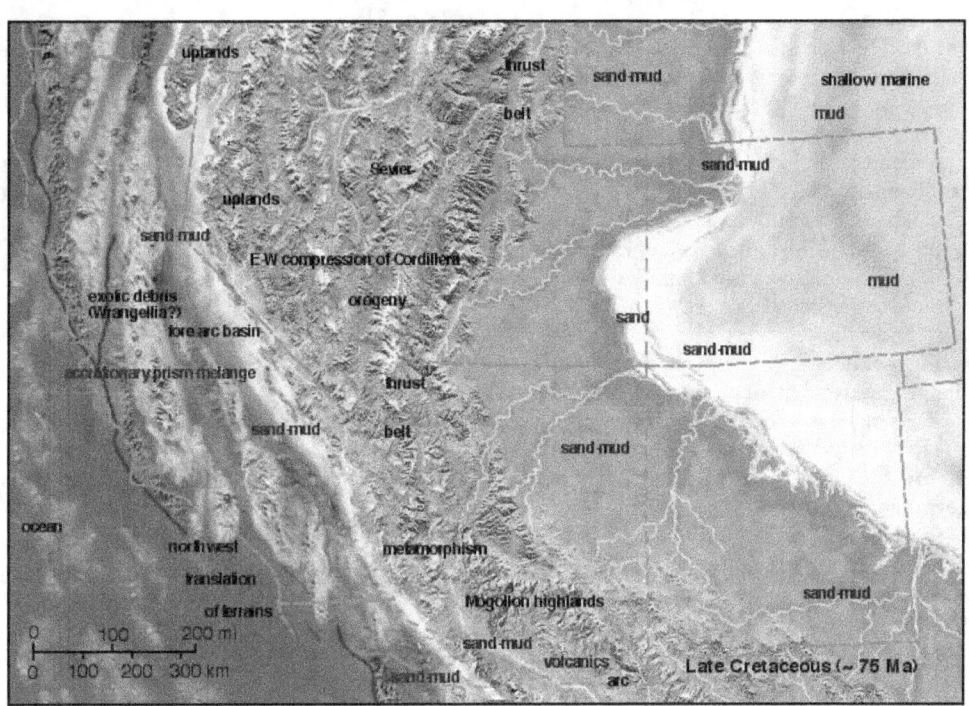

Figure 156B. Map of streams in the Walnut Canon area flowing into the interior seaway. Map courtesy of Dr. Ron Blakey, Northern Arizona University, http://jan.ucc.nau.edu/~rcb7/crepaleo.html, (Accessed March 2007).

Glossary

This glossary contains brief definitions of technical geologic terms used in this report. Not all geologic terms used are referenced. For more detailed definitions or to find terms not listed here please visit: http://wrgis.wr.usgs.gov/docs/parks/misc/glossarya.html.

aeolian. Formed, eroded, or deposited by or related to the action of the wind.

alluvial fan. A fan- shaped deposit of sediment that accumulates where a high gradient stream flows out of a mountain front into an area of lesser gradient such as a valley.

alluvium. Stream- deposited sediment that is generally rounded, sorted, and stratified.

aquifer. Rock or sediment that are sufficiently porous, permeable, and saturated to be useful as a source of water.

ash (volcanic). Fine pyroclastic material ejected from a volcano.

basin (structural). A doubly- plunging syncline in which rocks dip inward from all sides (also see dome).

basin (sedimentary). Any depression, from continental to local scales, into which sediments are deposited.

block (fault). A crustal unit bounded by faults, either completely or in part.

clastic. Rock or sediment made of fragments or pre-existing rocks.

clay. Clay minerals or sedimentary fragments the size of clay minerals (<2 cm).

continental crust. The type of crustal rocks underlying the continents and continental shelves; having a thickness of 25- 60 km (16- 37 mi) and a density of approximately 2.7 grams per cubic centimeter.

cross-bedding. Uniform to highly- varied sets of inclined sedimentary beds deposited by wind or water that indicate distinctive flow conditions.

crust. The outermost compositional shell of Earth, 10- 40 km (6- 25 mi) thick, consisting predominantly of relatively low- density silicate minerals (also see oceanic crust and continental crust).

deformation. A general term for the process of faulting, folding, shearing, extension, or compression of rocks as a result of various Earth forces.

dip. The angle between a structural surface and a horizontal reference plane measured normal to their line of intersection.

drainage basin. The total area from which a stream system receives or drains precipitation runoff.

dune. A low mound or ridge of sediment, usually sand, deposited by wind.

entrenched meander. An incised meander carved downward into the surface of the valley in which the meander originally formed.

epicontinental. Situated on the continental shelf or on the continental interior, as an epicontinental sea.

extrusive. Of or pertaining to the eruption of igneous material onto the surface of Earth.

fault. A subplanar break in rock along which relative movement occurs between the two sides.

formation. Fundamental rock- stratigraphic unit that is mappable and lithologically distinct from adjoining strata and has definable upper and lower contacts.

foreset. Pertaining to or forming a steep and advancing frontal slope, or the sediments deposited on such a slope.

graben. A down- dropped structural block bounded by steeply- dipping, normal faults (also see horst).

horst. An uplifted structural block bounded by high-angle normal faults.

igneous. Refers to a rock or mineral that originated from molten material; one of the three main classes or rocks: igneous, metamorphic, and sedimentary.

intrusion. A body of igneous rock that invades older rock. The invading rock may be a plastic solid or magma that pushes its way into the older rock.

island arc. A line or arc of volcanic islands formed over and parallel to a subduction zone.

joint. A semi- planar break in rock without relative movement of rocks on either side of the fracture surface.

lacustrine. Pertaining to, produced by, or inhabiting a lake or lakes.

lava. Magma that has been extruded out onto Earth's surface, both molten and solidified.

lineament. Any relatively straight surface feature that can be identified via observation, mapping, or remote sensing, often representing tectonic features.

lithology. The description of a rock or rock unit, especially the texture, composition, and structure of sedimentary rocks.

lithosphere. The relatively rigid outmost shell of Earth's structure, 50 to 100 km (31 to 62 mi) thick, that encompasses the crust and uppermost mantle.

magma. Molten rock generated within Earth that is the parent of igneous rocks.

mantle. The zone of Earth's interior between crust and core.

meanders. Sinuous lateral curves or bends in a stream's channel.

member. A lithostratigraphic unit with definable contacts that subdivides a formation.

mesa. A broad, flat- topped erosional hill or mountain that is bounded by steeply- sloping sides or cliffs.

monocline. A one- limbed flexure in strata, which are usually flat- lying except in the flexure itself.

normal fault. A dip- slip fault in which the hanging wall moves down relative to the footwall.

oceanic crust. Earth's crust formed at spreading ridges that underlies the ocean basins. Oceanic crust is 6- 7 km (3- 4 mi) thick and generally of basaltic composition.

orogeny. A mountain- building event, particularly a well-recognized event in the geological past (e.g. the Laramide orogeny).

outcrop. Any part of a rock mass or formation that is exposed or "crops out" at Earth's surface.

Pangaea. A theoretical, single supercontinent that existed during the Permian and Triassic Periods (also see Laurasia and Gondwana).

plateau. A broad, flat- topped topographic high of great extent and elevation above the surrounding plains, canyons, or valleys (both land and marine landforms).

pluton. A body of intrusive igneous rock.

point bar. A sand and gravel ridge deposited in a stream channel on the inside of a meander where flow velocity slows.

radiometric age. An age in years determined from radioisotopes and their decay products.

recharge. Infiltration processes that replenish groundwater.

regression. A long- term seaward retreat of the shoreline or relative fall of sea level.

reverse fault. A compressional, high angle (>45°), dip-slip fault in which the hanging wall moves up relative to the footwall (also see thrust fault).

ripple marks. The undulating, subparallel, usually small-scale, ridge pattern formed on sediment by the flow of wind or water.

sabkha. A coastal environment in an arid climate where evaporation rates are high.

sandstone. Clastic sedimentary rock of predominantly sand- sized grains.

sediment. An eroded and deposited, unconsolidated accumulation of lithic and mineral fragments.

shale. A clastic sedimentary rock made of clay- sized particles that exhibit parallel splitting properties.

silt. Clastic sedimentary material intermediate in size between fine- grained sand and coarse clay (1/256- 1/16 mm).

siltstone. A variable- lithified sedimentary rock with silt- sized grains.

stratigraphy. The geologic study of the origin, occurrence, distribution, classification, correlation, age, etc. of rock layers, especially sedimentary rocks.

strike. The compass direction of the line of intersection that an inclined surface makes with a horizontal plane.

strike-slip fault. A fault with measurable offset where the relative movement is parallel to the strike of the fault.

subduction zone. A convergent plate boundary where oceanic lithosphere descends beneath a continental or oceanic plate and is carried down into the mantle.

tectonic. Relating to large- scale movement and deformation of Earth's crust.

terraces (stream). Step- like benches surrounding the present floodplain of a stream due to dissection of previous flood plain(s), stream bed(s), and/or valley floor(s).

thrust fault. A dip- slip fault with a shallowly dipping fault surface (<45°) where the hanging wall moves up and over relative to the footwall.

trace fossils. Sedimentary structures, such as tracks, trails, burrows, etc., that preserve evidence of organisms' life activities, rather than the organisms themselves.

transgression. Landward migration of the sea due to a relative rise in sea level.

trend. The direction or azimuth of elongation or a linear geological feature.

unconformity. A surface within sedimentary strata that marks a prolonged period of nondeposition or erosion.

vent. An opening at the surface of Earth where volcanic materials emerge.

volcanic. Related to volcanoes; describes igneous rock crystallized at or near Earth's surface (e.g., lava).

water table. The upper surface of the saturated (phreatic) zone.

weathering. The set of physical, chemical, and biological processes by which rock is broken down in place.

References

This section provides a listing of references cited in this report. A more complete geologic bibliography is available and can be obtained through the NPS Geologic Resources Division.

Anderson, J. Lawford. 1988. Core Complexes of the Mojave- Sonoran Desert: Conditions of Plutonism, Mylonitization, and Decompression. In *Metamorphism and Crustal Evolution of the Western United States*, edited by W.G. Ernst. Englewood Cliffs, N.J.: Prentice Hall, 502- 525.

Anderson, Thomas H., and Jonathan A. Nourse. 2005. Pull- apart basins at releasing bends of the sinistral Late Jurassic Mojave- Sonora fault system. Boulder: Geological Society of America, Special Paper – 393, 97- 122.

Appel, Cynthia L., and Donald J. Bills. 1980. Map showing ground- water conditions in the Canyon Diablo Area, Coconino and Navajo Counties, Arizona – 1979. U.S. Geological Survey, Water- Resources Investigations, Open- File Report 80- 747, scale 1:250,000.

Biek, Robert F., Grant C. Willis, Michael D. Hylland, and Hellmut H. Doelling. 2000. Geology of Zion National Park, Utah. In *Geology of Utah's Parks and Monuments*, edited by Douglas A. Sprinkel, Thomas C. Chidsey, Jr., and Paul B. Anderson. Salt Lake City: Utah Geological Association Publication 28, 107- 138.

Billingsley, George H. 1989. Mesozoic Strata at Lees Ferry, Arizona. In *Centennial Field Guide*, edited by S. Beus. Denver: Rocky Mountain Section of the Geological Society of America, Vol. 2, 67- 71.

Billingsley, G.H., and H.M. Hampton. 2000. Geologic Map of the Grand Canyon 30' x 60' Quadrangle, Coconino and Mohave Counties, Northwestern Arizona. U.S. Geological Survey Geologic Investigations Series I- 2688, scale 1:100,000, http://pubs.usgs.gov/imap/i- 2688, (accessed May 2006), 15 p.

Billingsley, G.H., and J.L. Wellmeyer. 2002. Geologic Map of the Mount Trumball 30' x 60' Quadrangle, Mohave and Coconino Counties, northwest Arizona: USGS Geologic Investigations Series I- 2766, scale 1:100,000, http://pubs.usgs.gov/imap/i2766, (accessed October 2005), 30 p.

Bills, D.J., M. Truini, M.E. Flynn, H.A. Pierce, R.D. Catchings, and M.J. Rymer. 2000. Hydrogeology of the regional aquifer near Flagstaff, Arizona, 1994- 97. U.S. Geological Survey, Water- Resources Investigations Report 00- 4122, 143 p.

Christiansen, Eric H., Bart J. Kowallis, and Mark D. Barton. 1994. Temporal and spatial distribution of volcanic ash in Mesozoic sedimentary rocks of the Western Interior: an alternative record of Mesozoic magmatism. In *Mesozoic Systems of the Rocky Mountain Region, USA*, edited by Mario V. Caputo, James A. Peterson, and Karen J. Franczyk. Denver: Rocky Mountain Section, SEPM (Society for Sedimentary Geology), p. 73- 94.

Chronic, Halka. 1983. *Roadside Geology of Arizona*. Missoula: Mountain Press Publishing Company, p. 306- 307.

Dickinson, William R. 1981. Plate Tectonic Evolution of the Southern Cordillera: Tucson: Arizona Geological Society Digest, Vol. 14, 113- 135.

Dickinson, William R., and Timothy F. Lawton. 2001. Tectonic setting and sandstone petrofacies of the Bisbee Basin (USA- Mexico). Oxford: Journal of South American Earth Sciences, Vol. 14, Issue 5, 474- 504.

Dubiel, Russell F. 1994. Triassic deposystems, paleogeography, and paleoclimate of the Western Interior In *Mesozoic Systems of the Rocky Mountain Region, USA*, edited by Mario V. Caputo, James A. Peterson, and Karen J. Franczyk. Denver: Rocky Mountain Section, SEPM (Society for Sedimentary Geology), 133- 168.

Elder, William P., and James I. Kirkland. 1994. Cretaceous paleogeography of the Southern Western Interior Region. In *Mesozoic Systems of the Rocky Mountain Region, USA*, edited by M. V. Caputo, J. A. Peterson, and K. J. Franczyk. Denver: Rocky Mountain Section, SEPM (Society for Sedimentary Geology), 415- 440.

Greco, Deanna. 2008. *On- Site Analysis of Rockfall Incident, Walnut Canyon National Monument*, NPS Geologic Resources Division Official Memorandum to Walnut Canyon National Monument, Arizona. January 15, 2008

Haenggi, Water T., and William R. Muehlberger. 2005. Chihuahua Trough; a Jurassic pull- apart basin. Boulder: Geological Society of America, Special Paper – 393, 619- 630.

Hamblin, W.K. 2003. Late Cenozoic lava dams in the Western Grand Canyon. In *Grand Canyon Geology*, edited by S.S. Beus and M. Morales. New York: Oxford University Press, 2nd edition, 313- 345.

Hansen, Monica, Janet Coles, Kathryn A. Thomas, Daniel Cogan, Marion Reid, Jim Von Loh, and Keith Schulz. 2004. USGS- NPS Vegetation Mapping Program: Walnut Canyon National Monument, Arizona, Vegetation Classification and Distribution. Flagstaff: U.S. Geological Survey, Southwest Biological Science Center, Final Report, http://biology.usgs.gov/npsveg/waca/report.pdf, (accessed March 23, 2007), 130 p.

Henkle, W.R. 1976. Geology and engineering geology of eastern Flagstaff, Coconino County, Arizona. Flagstaff: Northern Arizona University, Master's Thesis, 123 p.

Hoffman, Paul F. 1989. Precambrian geology and tectonic history of North America. In *The Geology of North America: An Overview*, edited by Albert W. Bally and Allison R. Palmer. Boulder: Geological Society of America, The Geology of North America, Vol. A, 447- 512.

Hopkins, Ralph Lee and Kelcy J. Thompson. 2003. Kaibab Formation. In *Grand Canyon Geology*, edited by Stanley S. Beus and Michael Morales. New York: Oxford University Press, 2nd edition, p. 225- 246.

Huntoon, P.W. 2003. Post- Precambrian tectonism in the Grand Canyon region, In *Grand Canyon Geology*, edited by Stanley S. Beus and Michael Morales. New York: Oxford University Press, 2nd edition, 222- 259.

Karlstrom, K.E., B.R. Ilg, M.L. Williams, D.P. Hawkins, S.A. Bowring, and S.J. Seaman. 2003. Paleoproterozoic Rocks of the Granite Gorges. In *Grand Canyon Geology*, edited by S.S. Beus and M. Morales. New York: Oxford University Press, 2nd edition, 9- 38.

Lawton, Timothy F. 1994. Tectonic setting of Mesozoic sedimentary basins, Rocky Mountain region, United States. In *Mesozoic Systems of the Rocky Mountain Region, USA*, edited by Mario V. Caputo, James A. Peterson, and Karen J. Franczyk. Denver: Rocky Mountain Section, SEPM (Society for Sedimentary Geology), 1- 26.

Lucchitta, I. 2003. History of the Grand Canyon and of the Colorado River in Arizona. In *Grand Canyon Geology*, edited by S.S. Beus and M. Morales. New York: Oxford University Press, 2nd edition, 260- 274.

Lucchitta, I., and Jeanne, R.A. 2001. Geomorphic Features and Processes of the Shivwits Plateau, Arizona, and their Constraints on the Age of Western Grand Canyon. In *Colorado River: Origin and Evolution; Proceedings of a symposium held at Grand Canyon National Park in June, 2000*, edited by R.A. Young and E.E. Spamer. Grand Canyon: Grand Canyon Association, Monograph 12, 65- 70.

Luedke, R.G., and R.L. Smith. 1991. Quaternary volcanism in the western conterminous United States. In *Quaternary Nonglacial Geology: Conterminous U.S.*, edited by Roger B. Morrison. Boulder: The Geological Society of America, The Geology of North America Vo. K- 2, 75- 92.

Marshak, S., K. Karlstorm, and J.M. Timmons. 2000. Inversion of Proterozoic extensional faults: An explanation for the pattern of Laramide and Ancestral Rockies intracratonic deformation, United States: Boulder: *Geological Society of America Bulletin*, Vol. 28, 735- 738.

McCormack, D.C. 1989. The Geology of Wupatki National Monument, Northern Arizona. Flagstaff: Northern Arizona University, Master's Thesis, 97 p., 1 plate.

Middleton, Larry T., David K. Elliott, and Michael Morales. 2003. Coconino Sandstone In *Grand Canyon Geology*, edited by Stanley S. Beus and Michael Morales. New York: Oxford University Press, 2nd edition, 163- 179.

Morales, M. 2003. Mesozoic and Cenozoic strata of the Colorado Plateau near the Grand Canyon. In *Grand Canyon Geology*, edited by S.S. Beus and M. Morales. New York: Oxford University Press, 2nd edition, 212- 221.

Morris, Thomas H., Vicky W. Manning, and Scott M. Ritter. 2000. Geology of Capitol Reef National Park, Utah. In *Geology of Utah's Parks and Monuments*, edited by Douglas A. Sprinkel, Thomas C. Chidsey, Jr., and Paul B. Anderson. Salt Lake City: Utah Geological Association, Publication 28, 85- 106.

National Park Service. 1992. Draft natural and cultural resources management plan. Phoenix: National Park Service, Southern Arizona Group, 19 p.

National Park Service. 2003. Draft Environmental Impact Statement General Management Plan, Walnut Canyon National Monument, Arizona. Flagstaff: U.S. Department of Interior, National Park Service, http://planning.nps.gov/document/ACF247.pdf, (accessed December 2005), 204 p.

Noble, David Grant. 1991. *Ancient Ruins of the Southwest*. Flagstaff: Northland Publishing Company, 153- 155.

Oldow, John S., Albert W. Bally, Hans G. Ave Lallemant, and William P. Leeman. 1989. Phanerozoic evolution of the North American Cordillera; United States and Canada. In *The Geology of North America: An Overview*, edited by Albert W. Bally and Allison R. Palmer. Boulder: Geological Society of America, The Geology of North America, Vol. A, 139- 233.

Pallister, John S., and Edward A. du Bray. 1997. Interpretive Map and Guide to the Volcanic Geology of Chiricahua National Monument and Vicinity, Cochise County, Arizona. U.S. Geological Survey, Miscellaneous Investigations Series Map I- 2541, scale 1:24,000.

Peterson, James A. 1980. Permian paleogeography and sedimentary provinces, west central United States. In *Paleozoic Paleogeography of the West- Central United States*, edited by Thomas D. Fouch and Esther R. Magathan. Denver: Rocky Mountain Section, SEPM (Society for Sedimentary Geology), 271- 292.

Phillips, B.G. 1990. Riparian inventory of Walnut Canyon National Monument. Tucson: Southwest Parks and Monuments Association report, unpaginated.

Priest, Susan S., Wendell A. Duffield, Karen Malis- Clark, James W. Hendley II, and Peter H. Stauffer. 2001. The San Francisco Volcanic Field, Arizona. U.S. Geological Survey Fact Sheet 017- 01, http://geopubs.wr.usgs.gov/fact- sheet/fs017- 01, (accessed March 2007), 2 p.

Raucci, Jason, Michael Ort, Ronald C. Blakey, Paul J. Umhoefer, Nathan O. Blythe, and Mark Manone. 2004. National Park Service geologic resource evaluation; geologic mapping of Walnut Canyon National Monument and Petrified Forest National Park, northern Arizona. Boulder: Geological Society of America, Abstracts with Programs, Vol. 36, 230.

Raup, David M. 1991. *Extinction: Bad Genes or Bad Luck?* New York: W.W. Norton and Company, 210 p.

Rice, D.D., and G.W. Shurr. 1983. Patterns of sedimentation and paleogeography across the Western Interior Seaway during time of deposition of Upper Cretaceous Eagle Sandstone and equivalent rocks, northern Great Plains. In Mesozoic Paleogeography of the West- Central United States, edited by Mitchell W. Reynolds and Edward D. Dolly. SEPM (Society for Sedimentary Geology), Rocky Mountain Section, 337- 358.

Rowlands, Peter G., Charles C. Avery, Nancy J. Brian, and Heidemarie Johnson. 1995. Historical flow regimes and canyon bottom vegetation dynamics at Walnut Canyon National Monument, Arizona: prepared for Water Rights Branch, Water Resources Division, National Park Service, Fort Collins, Colorado, 107 p.

Santucci, Vincent L. and V. Luke Santucci, Jr.. 1999. An inventory of paleontological resources from Walnut Canyon National Monument, Arizona. In National Park Service Paleontological Research. Vol. 4. Edited by Vincent L. Santucci and Lindsay McClelland. GRD Technical Report NPS/NRGRD/GRDTR- 99/03, p. 118- 120.

Schroeder, A.H. 1977. *Of men and volcanoes: the Sinagua of northern Arizona*. Tucson: Southwest Parks and Monuments Association, 70 p.

Scott, William E. 2004. Quaternary volcanism in the United States. In *The Quaternary Period in the United States*, edited by A.R. Gillespie, S.C. Porter, and B.F. Atwater. San Francisco: Elsevier, Developments in Quaternary Science, 1, 351- 380.

Silberling, N. J. and R.J. Roberts. 1962. Pre- Tertiary stratigraphy and structure of northwestern Nevada. Boulder: Geological Society of America, Special Paper 72, 58 p.

Spencer, J.E., L. Peters, W.C. McIntosh, and P.J. Patchett. 2001. 40Ar/39Ar Geochronology of the Hualapai Limestone and Bouse Formation and Implications for the Age of the Lower Colorado River. In *Colorado River: Origin and Evolution; Proceedings of a symposium held at Grand Canyon National Park in June, 2000*, edited by R.A. Young and E.E. Spamer. Grand Canyon: Grand Canyon Association, Monograph 12, 89- 92.

Stewart, J.H., F. G. Poole, and R. F. Wilson. 1972. Stratigraphy and origin of the Triassic Moenkopi formation and related strata in the Colorado Plateau region with a section on sedimentary petrology by R.A. Cadigan. Denver: U.S. Geological Survey, Prof Paper 691, 195 p.

Thomas, Blakemore E. 2003. Water- quality data for Walnut Canyon and Wupatki National Monuments, Arizona – 2001- 02. Denver: U.S. Geological Survey, Open File Report 03- 286, 13 p.

Turner, Christine E. 2003. Toroweap Formation. In *Grand Canyon Geology*, edited by Stanley S. Beus and Michael Morales. New York: Oxford University Press, 2nd edition, 180- 195.

Vandiver, Vincent W. 1936. Geological report on Walnut Canyon National Monument, Arizona. National Park Service report, 12 p. and 3 photographs.

Whitefield, Paul. 2005. WACA Riparian Corridor Change interdisciplinary funding proposal, National Park Service, Flagstaff, Arizona. Written communication, November 30, 2005.

Appendix A: Geologic Map Graphic

The following page provides a preview or "snapshot" of the geologic map for Walnut Canyon National Monument. For a poster size PDF of this map or for digital geologic map data, please see the included CD or visit the GRE publications webpage: http://www2.nature.nps.gov/geology/inventory/gre_publications.cfm

Appendix B: Scoping Summary

The following excerpts are from the GRE scoping summary for Walnut Canyon National Monument. The scoping meeting occurred June 28- 29, 2001; therefore, the contact information and Web addresses referred to herein may be outdated. Please contact the Geologic Resources Division for current information.

Summary

A geologic resources inventory workshop was held for the three Flagstaff area NPS units (Walnut Canyon NM, Wupatki NM, Sunset Crater NM) on June 28th and 29th, 2001, to view and discuss the park's geologic resources, to address the status of geologic mapping for compiling both paper and digital maps, and to assess resource management issues and needs. Cooperators from the NPS Geologic Resources Division (GRD), NPS Flagstaff area office, Colorado State University, and United States Geologic Survey (USGS) were present for the workshop. This was part of a multi- park scoping session also involving Petrified Forest NP, Pipe Spring NM, and Navajo NM.

On Friday June 29th, scoping involved a half- day field trip to view the geology of Sunset Crater NM and Wupatki NM, led by Sarah Hanson (Adrian College) and Helen Fairley (NPS). On June 28th scoping included another half- day session to present overviews of the NPS Inventory and Monitoring (I&M) program, the Geologic Resources Division, and the on- going Geologic Resources Inventory (GRI). Round table discussions involving geologic issues for Flagstaff area parks included interpretation, natural resources, the status of geologic mapping efforts, sources of available data, geologic hazards, and action items generated from this meeting.

Currently, the major geologic issues facing the Flagstaff area parks are as follows:
- acquiring digital geologic maps at a large scale suitable for resource management needs;
- production of an interpretive product that could be sold in visitor centers showcasing the geologic map of each area and its significance to the other resources;
- evaluating potential volcanic hazards in the Flagstaff area and how they might affect park resources, and
- an inventory of the paleontological resources at each park.

The meeting attendees for the Walnut Canyon National Monument session are listed at the end of this appendix.

Geologic Mapping

All three Flagstaff area parks are included on the USGS publication *Map Showing Geology, Structure, and Uranium Deposits of the Flagstaff 1 x 2 degree quadrangle, Arizona* (USGS Map I- 1446, scale 1:250,000). While this small scale is not necessarily conducive for resource management, it is an excellent compilation map and was developed based upon larger scale mapping. However,

larger scale mapping (at least 1:24,000 scale) is desirable for each of the three parks.

Also, the USGS published the *Geologic Map of the Eastern San Francisco volcanic field, Arizona* (USGS Map I- 953, scale of 1:50,000) that also covers the areas of the three parks, but the map does not necessarily include geologic mapping of each park. Specifically, the only park that is fully covered on this sheet is Sunset Crater NM. Walnut Canyon NM is completely uncovered and Wupatki NM is only partially covered.

Park staff were interested in seeing a map showing travertine deposits because it has numerous implications for the cultural significance in population distributions and the history of water in the area, so it should be a component of any new mapping.

Additionally, volcanic- and other features should be included (vents, flows, lava tubes, ice caves, etc.) as they are important in deducing a potential for volcanic hazards in the area as well as providing baseline data for what types of features exist in the park.

Digital Geologic Map coverage: It is not known if any of the USGS maps (I- 953 and I- 1446) for the area have been converted to a digital format. If they have not it is suggested that they be scanned, registered and rectified for preliminary use in a GIS until new mapping is accomplished as they are the best available source of baseline geologic data for each park.

Other Desired GIS Data

Nicole Tancreto had served as the Flagstaff GIS support person, but is now in a GIS position for the Southern Colorado Plateau network. She mentioned at the meeting that the boundary for Walnut Canyon NM was incorrect on our maps, so she supplied GRI staff with the correct boundary as ESRI shape files.

Aerial photography is desired for the entire area and would assist in any future needed geologic mapping. It was suggested to contact the Vegetation Mapping program and the USFS to see if they have such data for the area.

Miscellaneous Items of Interest

Current natural resource staff at Flagstaff area parks are Helen Fairley (archeologist), Paul Whitefield, and Todd Metzger.

Geothermal development is a hot topic for the Flagstaff area, and could have effects on each parks management plan. Geothermal development was not noted as an issue for Walnut Canyon National Monument.

Walnut Canyon National Monument

- General geology of WACA consists of the Kaibab, Toroweap, Coconino, Moenkopi formations, as well as some igneous cinders.
- I- 953 does not cover the geology of WACA, and thus a large- scale geologic map is definitely needed.
- Paleontological resources do exist in exposures along WACA trails and have been subjected to pilferage over

the years. A paleontological survey is advised for the park.
- Detailed studies of the alluvial deposits in the canyons are desired. Richard Hereford (USGS) is the most likely qualified candidate to do this and should be consulted for his interest
- George Billingsley mentioned that there is a dam in the park that should be restored and incorporated into the parks interpretive story.

Name	Affiliation	Phone	E- Mail
Tim Connors	NPS, GRD	303- 969- 2093	Tim_Connors@nps.gov
Helen Fairley	NPS, Flagstaff area	928- 526- 1157	Helen_fairley@nps.gov
John Graham	Colorado State Univ.	970- 225- 6333	rockdoc250@comcast.net
Sarah Hanson	SUCR GIP	520- 526- 0502 517- 264- 3944	Slhanson@adrian.edu
Paul Whitefield	NPS, Flagstaff area	928- 526- 1157	Paul_whitefield@nps.gov

Walnut Canyon National Monument
Geologic Resource Evaluation Report

Natural Resource Report NPS/NRPC/GRD/NRR—2008/040
NPS D-38, June 2008

National Park Service
Director • Mary A. Bomar

Natural Resource Stewardship and Science
Acting Associate Director • Mary Foley, Chief Scientist of the Northeast Region

Natural Resource Program Center
The Natural Resource Program Center (NRPC) is the core of the NPS Natural Resource Stewardship and Science Directorate. The Center Director is located in Fort Collins, with staff located principally in Lakewood and Fort Collins, Colorado and in Washington, D.C. The NRPC has five divisions: Air Resources Division, Biological Resource Management Division, Environmental Quality Division, Geologic Resources Division, and Water Resources Division. NRPC also includes three offices: The Office of Education and Outreach, the Office of Inventory, Monitoring and Evaluation, and the Office of Natural Resource Information Systems. In addition, Natural Resource Web Management and Partnership Coordination are cross- cutting disciplines under the Center Director. The multidisciplinary staff of NRPC is dedicated to resolving park resource management challenges originating in and outside units of the national park system.

Geologic Resources Division
Chief • Dave Steensen
Planning Evaluation and Permits Branch Chief • Carol McCoy

Credits
Author • John Graham
Review • Lisa Norby and Carol McCoy
Editing • Trista Thornberry- Ehrlich, Sid Covington, and Melanie Ransmeier
Digital Map Production • Anne Poole
Map Layout Design • Andrea Croskrey